ESSENTIAL GUIDES FOR SUCCESSFUL PARENTING

MARIWAN HASAN

Made with ♥ on the Notion Press Platform
www.notionpress.com

This book is dedicated to every parent who has ever felt the weight of the world on their shoulders, juggling the demands of career, family, and the ever-evolving landscape of modern life. It is dedicated to those who strive to do their best, even when they stumble and fall. To those who question their abilities, doubt their choices, and yearn for a deeper connection with their children. This is for the parents who are exhausted but unwavering, who love fiercely despite the challenges, and who are willing to learn and grow alongside their children. It is a testament to the resilience of the human spirit, the unwavering power of parental love, and the hope that we can all find our way toward creating healthier,

happier families. This is for those parents who are searching for a better way, for a path that leads not just to financial success, but to a profound and lasting connection with the most important people in their lives—their children. For the parents who, despite the cracks, choose to rebuild, to repair, and to create a future built on love, understanding, and meaningful connection. This is for you.

Contents

Foreword

Essential Guides for Successful Parenting is not about pointing fingers or assigning blame. It's about fostering understanding and providing a practical guide for navigating the complex world of modern parenting. We live in an era of unprecedented pressures, where financial stability, career success, and the demands of technology often overshadow the most critical aspect of raising children: nurturing their emotional well-being. This book delves into the subtle yet profound consequences of neglecting this crucial element, exploring the various ways in which well-intentioned yet misguided approaches can lead to long-term negative impacts. We'll examine the pervasive influence of screens, the pitfalls of overly permissive

parenting, and the dangers of outsourcing crucial parenting tasks to technology. We'll discuss the importance of mindful parenting, the power of unconditional love, and the necessity of creating a safe and supportive family environment. But more importantly, we will equip parents with the tools and strategies they need to build strong, healthy relationships with their children. Throughout the book, you'll encounter relatable scenarios and compelling examples illustrating the subtle ways in which even the most loving parents can inadvertently create *Beyond the Cracks of Care* in their child's foundation. We will explore how to identify the warning signs of these cracks, discuss effective methods for mending them, and ultimately, build a strong and resilient future for our children. Remember, this journey is not about perfection; it is about progress. It is about embracing the challenges, learning from our mistakes, and striving to become the best parents we can be.

Preface

As a parenting expert and one who cares about child psychology with a background in fiction writing, I've spent years observing the dynamics of family life in all its complexities. The origin of this bookstems from a deep concern about the subtle yet significant shifts in modern parenting practices. The relentless pressures of contemporary society—financial insecurity, career demands, the pervasive influence of technology—often lead to well-intentioned parents adopting strategies that inadvertently undermine the very foundation of their children's emotional well-being. In countless consultations and through anecdotal observations, I've witnessed the profound impact of neglecting emotional connection in favor of material provision, or of allowing screens to replace meaningful interaction. This book is not intended as a judgment, but rather an empathetic exploration of these challenges. It is a call to action, an invitation to reflect on our parenting styles, to examine the potential cracks in our approach, and to actively work towards nurturing a healthier, more fulfilling parent-child relationship. I believe that by understanding the root causes of these issues and embracing mindful parenting techniques, we can create a supportive environment where children flourish, both emotionally and academically. Within these pages, you will find practical strategies, relatable examples, and a framework for rebuilding those foundational connections that are so crucial for a child's successful development.

ONE

THE MODERN PARENTING PARADOX

The relentless hum of the modern world often drowns out the quiet cries of our children. We live in a society that glorifies achievement, quantifies success, and measures worth in dollar signs. This relentless pursuit of the "ideal" –the bigger house, the better car, the prestigious career – has inadvertently created a chasm between parents and their children, a subtle fracture in the foundation of family life.

We're so busy building our empires that we often fail to notice the cracks forming in the very structures we're striving to protect: our families.

This paradox is at the heart of modern parenting. We strive to provide our children with every material advantage, believing that financial security equates to a happy childhood. We fill their lives with toys, gadgets, and expensive experiences, yet somehow, something feels...missing. The irony is profound: in our relentless pursuit of a secure future for our children, we inadvertently neglect their present emotional needs. We're drowning them in material possessions while starving them of genuine connection. This imbalance, this subtle disconnect, is what I call the Hidden Crack. It's the unseen fracture in the foundation of a child's emotional well-being, a hairline fissure that can, over time, widen into a devastating chasm.

The pressure cooker of modern life intensifies the paradox. Many parents struggle to balance the demands of high-powered careers with the responsibilities of raising a family. The expectation to succeed professionally while simultaneously providing attentive, nurturing care to children is often overwhelming, even impossible. The result is a feeling of constant inadequacy, a nagging sense that we're falling short, both as parents and as professionals. This constant pressure often leads to a reliance on quick fixes, shortcuts, and technological solutions that, while seemingly convenient, can erode the very essence of parenting.

The pervasive belief that financial success equals good parenting is a dangerous myth. While financial stability provides a crucial level of security, it is not a substitute for genuine connection, love, and emotional support. A child living in a mansion but starved of parental attention and genuine affection is not thriving; they are merely surviving. The abundance of material goods fails to compensate for the absence of a secure emotional environment. In fact, it often exacerbates the issue, creating a child who believes their worth is measured solely by external achievements and possessions, leading to an unhealthy sense of entitlement and a lack of self-worth.

Consider the scenario of a child whose parents are constantly working long hours, prioritizing their careers over family dinners or bedtime stories. The child, craving attention and connection, might act out, seeking validation through disruptive behavior. Their actions, however challenging, are desperate cries for connection, for the presence and attention of their parents. This, tragically, is often misconstrued as defiance or misbehavior, leading to further conflict and widening the "hidden crack" instead of mending it. The parent, burdened by work stress and societal pressures, might resort to technological solutions – handing the child an iPad or smartphone to keep them quiet. This momentary relief, however, comes at a significant cost.

Beyond the Cracks of Careisn't always a dramatic event. It's not a single, catastrophic failure, but a slow, insidious erosion of the parent-child bond. It's the consistent absence of genuine engagement, the subtle neglect of emotional needs, the

unspoken anxieties that simmer beneath the surface of a seemingly functional family. It's the reliance on technology to fill the void of parental presence, the prioritization of external validation over internal connection. It manifests in countless ways: the parent perpetually engrossed in their phone during family meals, the child spending hours alone in their room, the lack of meaningful conversations, the

absence of physical affection.

These seemingly minor omissions, these everyday instances of disconnection, accumulate over time, slowly eroding the child's sense of security, belonging, and self-worth. They leave behind a subtle but profound impact on a child's emotional well-being. The lack of consistent, empathetic parental guidance can manifest as anxiety, depression, difficulty forming healthy relationships, struggles with self-esteem, and a diminished sense of identity. The child might become withdrawn, overly aggressive, or excessively compliant, struggling to navigate the complexities of social interactions and emotional regulation. Academic performance can suffer, as the lack of emotional support and consistent encouragement impacts motivation and focus.

The consequences of *Beyond the Cracks of Care* can extend far beyond childhood. Children who experience consistent emotional neglect or a lack of meaningful connection with their parents are at increased risk of developing mental health issues, experiencing relationship difficulties, and facing challenges in their personal and professional lives as adults. The pattern of emotional disconnection can become deeply ingrained, affecting their ability to form healthy relationships, regulate their emotions, and achieve a sense of fulfillment in their lives. This is a sobering reality that highlights the profound importance of cultivating strong, nurturing parent-child relationships.

The modern parenting paradox is not about condemning parents; it's about acknowledging the immense pressures they face and offering support and guidance. It's not about judging, but about understanding. Many parents are genuinely trying their best, yet they are trapped in a system that often prioritizes external measures of success over internal well-being. This book is designed to help navigate the complexities of modern parenting, to identify the subtle signs of the "hidden crack," and to provide parents with tools and strategies to foster healthier, more fulfilling relationships with their children. It's a call to action, an invitation to reclaim the parent-child bond, and to build families based on genuine connection, unconditional love, and mutual respect, rather than on the often-misleading metrics of material success. The journey of parenthood is not a race, but a marathon that requires patience, understanding, and a relentless commitment to nurturing the emotional well-being of our children. The goal is not perfection, but progress. It's about creating a secure foundation, brick by brick, love by love and connection by connection. This is where we begin to heal the unseen fracture.

The Screen's Silent Influence

The glow of the screen, a seductive siren song in the modern home, often lulls parents into a false sense of security. It's the digital babysitter, the quiet entertainer, the readily available distraction. But behind its seemingly innocuous façade lies a silent influence, subtly reshaping the very fabric of a child's development. We, as parents, often fail to recognize the insidious creep of this influence, mistaking it for harmless entertainment or even a valuable educational tool. The truth, however, is far more nuanced and often unsettling.

The statistics are alarming, painting a picture of a generation shaking on the edge of a digital precipice. Studies consistently link excessive screen time to a significant increase in attention deficit disorders. The constant bombardment of stimuli, the rapid-fire transitions between images and sounds, overwhelms the developing brain, making it increasingly difficult to focus on single tasks, to maintain concentration, to filter out distractions. Children struggle to sit still, to listen attentively, to complete assignments. The screen, with its endless parade of flashing lights and immediate gratification, rewires the brain, prioritizing instant reward over sustained effort. This isn't simply about fidgeting; it's about a fundamental alteration in how the brain processes information, a shift that can have profound and lasting consequences.

Beyond the attention deficit, lies the chilling spectre of social isolation. The screen, while seemingly connecting children to a vast network of peers, paradoxically isolates them from genuine human interaction. The fleeting, superficial connections forged online often fail to satisfy the deep-seated human need for empathy, understanding, and shared experiences. Children immersed in the digital world learn to communicate through emojis and abbreviated texts, losing the crucial skills of nonverbal communication, active listening, and nuanced emotional expression. The subtleties of facial expressions, the rhythm of conversation, the art of compromise – these are skills learned not through pixels and screens, but through face-to-face interaction, through the messy, sometimes uncomfortable, yet essential process of building real-world relationships.

The emotional impact is perhaps the most concerning. The curated perfection of social media, the constant exposure to idealized versions of reality, fosters unrealistic expectations and fuels feelings of inadequacy. Children compare themselves to their online personas, often feeling like they fall short of the meticulously crafted images presented to them. This can lead to low self-esteem, anxiety, and depression. The relentless pressure to conform, to achieve, to project an image of flawless happiness, takes a heavy toll on the developing psyche. The screen becomes a mirror reflecting not their authentic selves, but a distorted version shaped by societal pressures and digital filters. The constant stream of negativity, cyberbullying, and exposure to inappropriate content further exacerbates these issues, creating a toxic environment that can deeply scar a young mind.

Sleep patterns, too, are profoundly affected. The blue light emitted from screens interferes with melatonin production, disrupting the body's natural sleep-wake cycle. Children who spend hours glued to screens often suffer from sleep deprivation, which in turn impacts their mood, concentration, and overall well-being. The cumulative effect of poor sleep, lack of focus, and emotional instability creates a vicious cycle, exacerbating the already existing challenges.

It's a silent erosion, a gradual chipping away at the foundations of a child's physical and mental health. The consequences are not always immediately apparent, but they accumulate over time, often manifesting as behavioral problems, academic struggles, and difficulties forming healthy relationships later in life.

The problem isn't technology itself; technology is a tool, and like any tool, it can be used constructively or destructively.

The issue lies in our relationship with technology, in our tendency to rely on screens as a convenient solution to the complex challenges of parenting. It's a societal issue, a reflection of our fast-paced, over-scheduled lives, where the allure of instant gratification and passive entertainment often overshadows the importance of genuine connection and mindful engagement. We must consciously reclaim our children's time, creating spaces and opportunities for unplugged play, for face-to-face interactions, for fostering the crucial skills necessary for navigating the complexities of life.

Consider the scenario of a family dinner. Instead of engaging in meaningful conversations, family members are often glued to their devices, a silent testament to the digital divide that's subtly fracturing family bonds. The shared meal, a time-honored tradition for connection and communication, becomes a solitary experience, each individual lost in their digital world. The laughter, the shared stories, the spontaneous moments of connection – these are replaced by the sterile glow of the screen, a chilling reminder of the silent influence technology holds over our lives.

Think about bedtime routines. Instead of comforting rituals and lullabies, the screen becomes the last thing a child sees before falling asleep. The blue light, the constant stimulation, interferes with the body's natural sleep cycle, impacting the child's ability to rest and recharge. The screen becomes a silent antagonist, undermining the very foundations of healthy development.

Even educational apps, while touted as valuable learning tools, often fail to replicate the richness and complexity of real-world experiences. The interactive nature of these apps, while engaging in the short term, can lead to a passive learning style, hindering the child's ability to think critically, to solve problems independently, to learn through trial and error. The screen, while offering a plethora of information, fails to provide the essential human element – the guidance, the support, the personalized interaction crucial for effective learning.

The challenge, therefore, lies not in eliminating technology altogether – an unrealistic and perhaps even undesirable goal in our increasingly digital world – but in cultivating a healthy and balanced relationship with it. We need to be mindful of our children's screen time, setting clear boundaries and establishing routines that prioritize face-to-face interaction, unplugged play, and meaningful engagement with the world around them. We need to model healthy technology use ourselves, showing our children that there is a world beyond the screen, a world that offers rich experiences, authentic connections, and opportunities for personal growth. We need to actively engage in our children's lives, providing them with the love, support, and guidance they need to thrive in a world increasingly dominated by technology.

It's a delicate dance, a balancing act between embracing the benefits of technology while mitigating its potential harms. It requires conscious effort, mindful parenting, and a commitment to prioritizing the emotional and physical well-being of our children above all else. The silent influence of the screen is a real and present danger, but it's a danger we can overcome with awareness, intention, and a renewed focus on the importance of genuine human connection. The crack might be silent, but its effects are far from subtle, and the healing begins with a conscious choice to reclaim our children's time and attention, a choice to nurture the parent-child bond above the flickering light of the digital world. It's a choice for a future where the screen doesn't dominate, but complements the rich tapestry of human experience. It's about building a future where our children's development is not shaped by the silent influence of the screen but nurtured by the warmth and guidance of a loving and present parent. It's a journey, not a destination, a commitment to a healthier, more fulfilling, and more deeply connected family life.

The Permissive Parenting Pitfall

The insidious nature of screen time, as we've discussed, is only one facet of the unseen fracture threatening the foundations of our children's well-being. Another, equally pervasive, and often interconnected, element is the pervasive pitfall of permissive parenting. This isn't about being a stern, unyielding disciplinarian; it's about recognizing the crucial role of boundaries, consequences, and consistent guidance in fostering a child's sense of security, self-reliance, and emotional maturity. Permissive parenting, in its extreme form, creates an environment where children are essentially untethered, lacking the necessary structure and support to navigate the complexities of life.

Imagine a child who has never experienced the frustration of delayed gratification. Every whim is met, every desire fulfilled. They want a sugary treat before dinner? No problem. They refuse to tidy their room? It's fine, the parent will do it. They want to stay up past their bedtime? The rules are flexible, easily bent to suit the child's preferences. This seemingly benevolent approach, born of good intentions – a desire to avoid conflict, to nurture a child's happiness –actually sows the seeds of insecurity and ultimately undermines the very development it seeks to protect.

The absence of boundaries creates a vacuum, a space where a child struggles to develop crucial self-regulatory skills. They lack the internal compass to guide their behavior, to differentiate between right and wrong, to understand the concept of cause and effect. The constant indulgence, the absence of consequences, doesn't nurture a feeling of security; instead, it breeds a pervasive anxiety. The child is never quite sure what is expected of them, leaving them adrift in a sea of uncertainty.

This uncertainty can manifest as behavioral problems, ranging from tantrums and defiance to more serious acts of aggression or self-harm. The lack of consistent guidance leaves them feeling lost, unable to navigate even minor challenges without resorting to emotional outbursts or manipulative behavior.

The result often isn't the carefree, happy child that permissive parenting aims to create, but rather a child fraught with anxiety, struggling with self-esteem, and ill-equipped to handle life's inevitable setbacks. This is not to say that all children raised in permissive environments will suffer these consequences. Resilience and inherent personality traits play a significant role. However, the risk is undeniably increased, and the potential long-term consequences are substantial.

The contrast between a permissive parenting style and a more balanced, nurturing approach is striking. Consider a child who, upon receiving a new toy, excitedly tears open the wrapping, only to discover it's broken. In a permissive environment, the response might be immediate replacement or a hasty effort to repair the damage, perhaps even an apology to the child for their disappointment. The child learns nothing about dealing with frustration, accepting disappointment, or understanding that not every situation has an easy fix. In contrast, a parent employing a more mindful approach might acknowledge the child's disappointment, validating their feelings while also offering an opportunity to learn. They might engage the child in problem-solving, discussing alternative ways to play with the damaged toy, or perhaps even suggesting they learn to repair it themselves. This fosters resilience, problem-solving skills, and a healthy understanding that disappointment is a part of life, and that challenges can be overcome.

This difference extends far beyond broken toys. Imagine a teenager struggling with academic performance. A permissive parent might simply lower their expectations, excusing the poor grades as a phase or a temporary setback.

They might even step in and complete assignments, or pressure teachers to offer leniency. This, however, deprives the teenager of the opportunity to learn from their mistakes, to develop responsibility for their academic success, and to cultivate the essential discipline needed for future success. A more balanced approach would involve working collaboratively with the teenager, identifying the underlying causes of the poor performance, developing strategies to improve, and setting realistic expectations and consequences for their actions. This fosters a sense of responsibility, self-reliance, and a deeper understanding of the importance of effort and perseverance.

The absence of consequences in a permissive parenting style also contributes to a sense of entitlement. Children who are constantly indulged, who are seldom challenged or required to accept any form of responsibility, often develop a sense of being entitled to what they want, regardless of the cost or effort involved. This entitlement can manifest in various ways, from demanding excessive attention to exhibiting rudeness and disrespect towards others. It can impact their relationships, making it difficult to develop empathy and appreciate the perspectives of others. This can lead to strained relationships with peers, family members, and later in life, even romantic partners and colleagues. They may struggle to form and maintain healthy relationships, as their sense of entitlement prevents them from compromising or considering the needs of others.

Moreover, the lack of clear expectations and boundaries can lead to significant problems in adulthood. Individuals raised in permissive environments may struggle with self- regulation, exhibiting impulsive behavior and difficulty controlling their emotions. This lack of self-control can impact every aspect of their lives, from their professional success to their personal relationships. They may struggle to maintain employment, manage finances responsibly, or navigate the complexities of adult relationships. This can lead to feelings of inadequacy, low self-esteem, and a profound sense of being lost or adrift in the world. They might turn to unhealthy coping mechanisms like substance abuse or excessive risk-taking to alleviate the underlying anxiety and sense of unease stemming from their lack of internal structure and guidance.

The key to avoiding the permissive parenting pitfall isn't about instilling fear or creating a rigid, authoritarian environment. It's about finding a balance – a delicate interplay between love, support, and consistent, age-appropriate boundaries. It's about fostering independence while providing the necessary guidance and support to help children develop the self-confidence and resilience they need to thrive. It's about teaching them self-discipline, not through punishment, but through understanding and empathy. It's about setting clear expectations, establishing consistent consequences, and helping children understand that their actions have consequences, both positive and negative. It's about empowering them to make good choices and learn from their mistakes, not by rescuing them from their consequences, but by supporting them as they navigate the challenges and learn to accept responsibility for their own actions. It's about raising individuals who are not only happy, but also resilient, responsible, and well-equipped to navigate the complexities of life.

This is not a task that can be accomplished overnight. It requires consistent effort, patience, and a willingness to adapt our parenting strategies as our children grow and Change.

It demands a deep understanding of child development, emotional intelligence, and a commitment to establishing a loving, supportive, and yet firmly structured home environment. The benefits, however, are immeasurable. By establishing clear boundaries and consistent consequences, we empower our children to develop the self-reliance, emotional intelligence, and responsible decision-making skills they'll need to thrive, not just as children, but as adults navigating the challenges and opportunities of life. The unseen fracture, the subtle erosion of a child's sense of security and self-reliance, can be prevented, not through indulgence, but through thoughtful, intentional parenting – a parenting style that prioritizes nurturing independence, fostering resilience, and equipping our children with the tools they need to navigate life's complex journey with confidence and grace. The investment in mindful, consistent parenting today is an investment in the well-being and success of our children tomorrow. It's a choice for a stronger, more secure, and ultimately more fulfilling future, for both parents and children alike. It is a journey that requires commitment, patience, and a deep understanding of the delicate balance between love and discipline, but one that yields immeasurable rewards in the years to come.

Delegation and Disengagement

The glowing screen hummed, a siren song lulling both parent and child into a false sense of security. It wasn't just the hours spent passively consuming content; it was the insidious creep of delegation, the subtle shift of responsibility from the nurturing embrace of a parent to the cold, impersonal algorithm of a device. We hand our children tablets to quiet them, pacify them, educate them —outsourcing the very essence of parenting to a glowing rectangle. We believe we're saving time, providing

enrichment, even fostering independence. But what are we truly accomplishing?

This isn't about demonizing technology. Technology, like fire, is a tool. Used wisely, it can be a powerful ally. But like fire, it can also consume us, leaving behind ashes where once a vibrant connection flourished. The problem lies not in the existence of screens, but in the disengagement they

enable, the insidious way they erode the crucial,

irreplaceable bond between parent and child.

Think about it: a child struggling with a complex math problem. Instead of patiently guiding them through the process, showing them the logic, fostering their problem-solving skills, we hand them a learning app. The app might provide the answer, but it won't provide the experience of collaborative learning, the shared joy of overcoming a challenge, the quiet pride in mastering a new concept under the watchful, loving guidance of a parent. This subtle shift represents a forfeiture of invaluable moments, a gradual weakening of the connection that underpins a child's emotional security.

Consider the bedtime story. The familiar rhythm of a parent's voice, the comforting cadence, the subtle nuances of inflection – these are not simply elements of a bedtime ritual; they are building blocks of emotional bonding. They forge a connection that transcends words, an unspoken language of love and security. Replacing this with a pre-recorded animation, no matter how sophisticated, diminishes the depth and intimacy of this crucial interaction. The child loses the warmth of physical proximity, the feeling of being fully seen and understood, the unspoken language of parental love that is communicated through touch, gaze, and the very presence of a loving caregiver.

And what about playtime? The spontaneous creativity of building a fort, the shared laughter of a silly game, the imaginative worlds conjured in a backyard – these are not mere diversions; they are the crucible where a child's social and emotional skills are honed. They are the foundations of empathy, cooperation, conflict resolution, and emotional regulation. Delegating playtime to screens, even interactive games, often lacks the spontaneity, the negotiation, the flexibility, and the unstructured learning that characterizes true, parent-led play. It replaces genuine human interaction with a programmed experience, limiting the child's ability to develop crucial social and emotional intelligence.

This disengagement isn't confined to the digital realm. It manifests in other ways, too. The parent who delegates all discipline to a school, the parent who outsources homework help to tutors, the parent who relies on babysitters or extended family for the majority of childcare—all of these represent a relinquishing of essential parental duties. While seeking outside help is often necessary and beneficial, the consistent delegation of crucial responsibilities weakens the parent-child bond and hinders the child's development. It's not about doing everything ourselves, but about actively participating, being present, and ensuring that the child's fundamental needs are met through direct engagement with a loving and supportive caregiver.

The consequences of this delegation and disengagement can be profound and far-reaching. Children who lack consistent parental involvement often struggle with emotional regulation, self-esteem, and social skills. They may exhibit behavioral problems, struggle academically, and experience difficulties forming healthy relationships. The absence of consistent guidance and support can lead to a sense of insecurity, a feeling of being unloved, or even neglected.

This isn't to say that every parent needs to be present at every moment; that's impossible and unrealistic. But it is crucial to be consistently and meaningfully present in the moments that matter most, ensuring that the child's needs are met not only materially, but also emotionally and psychologically.

The impact extends beyond childhood. Children raised with significant parental disengagement may struggle to form healthy adult relationships, experience challenges in the workplace, and have difficulty managing stress and conflict.

They may struggle with issues of trust, self-worth, and personal responsibility. This isn't about blaming parents; it's about recognizing the importance of active, engaged parenting in shaping a child's future trajectory. It's about understanding that the emotional bond forged in early childhood lays the foundation for a lifetime of healthy relationships and well-being.

The antidote to this pervasive disengagement lies in mindful presence, in making conscious choices to prioritize genuine connection over convenient delegation. It's about putting down the phone, turning off the screen, and actively engaging with our children, listening to their concerns, sharing their joys, and guiding them through the complexities of life. It's about creating opportunities for spontaneous connection, for unstructured play, for heartfelt conversations. It's about being present, not just physically, but emotionally and mentally. It's about rediscovering the profound joy of nurturing and guiding a child, not just overseeing their needs through the lens of a screen or a pre-programmed app.

This isn't a call for perfection, because parenting is rarely perfect. We all stumble, we all make mistakes. But the goal is to strive for intentionality, to consciously choose engagement over disengagement, connection over convenience. It's about creating a space where our children feel seen, heard, loved, and understood – a space where they can thrive, not just survive.

The technology itself is not the villain. The villain is the mindset that allows us to become passive observers in our children's lives. It's the gradual erosion of the parent-child bond, the slow relinquishing of responsibility to a system that cannot replace the irreplaceable warmth, wisdom, and unconditional love that only a parent can offer. It's the subtle fracturing of that vital connection, a crack that, left unaddressed, can cause irreparable damage to a child's emotional, social, and psychological well-being. Let's choose instead to actively cultivate those connections, those invaluable moments of shared experience, the building blocks of a strong and secure foundation upon which our children can build a happy and fulfilling life. The investment is not just in their future; it's an investment in our own well-being, in the creation of a loving and connected family – a bond far more valuable than any digital distraction. Let's reclaim the joy and responsibility of parenting, and nurture the irreplaceable connection that lies at its heart. Let's repair the unseen fracture before it irrevocably alters the course of a child's life. The power to heal lies not in technology, but in the conscious and deliberate choices we make each and every day. Let's choose wisely.

TWO
THE EROSION OF CONNECTION

The insidious erosion of connection doesn't happen overnight. It's a slow, almost imperceptible drift, like the steady retreat of the tide, leaving behind a landscape subtly altered, the once-firm foundation now subtly weakened. We, as parents, often become so preoccupied with the minutiae of daily life – the schedules, the errands, the endless to-do lists– that we fail to notice the quiet withdrawal, the subtle shift in our children's demeanor. The laughter might be less frequent, the shared confidences fewer, the comfortable silences replaced by a pervasive unease. These are the early warning signs, the faint cracks in the foundation of our relationships, often masked by the superficial normalcy of our daily routines.

It's not about the quantity of time spent with our children, but the quality. A fleeting glance across the dinner table, punctuated by hurried bites and distracted chatter, is not the same as a shared meal where eyes meet, stories are exchanged, and genuine connection is fostered. It's the difference between presence and mere proximity. We may be physically present in the same room, yet emotionally miles apart, lost in the vortex of our own thoughts and responsibilities. Our children, acutely sensitive to our emotional availability, absorb this disconnection, internalizing it as a reflection of their own worth. They learn, perhaps unconsciously, that their thoughts, feelings, and experiences are secondary to the demands of the adult world.

Consider the ubiquitous presence of technology. It's not simply the hours spent passively consuming content, but the constant, subtle intrusion into our shared moments. Even when we are physically present, our minds might be elsewhere, scrolling through social media feeds, checking emails, or responding to notifications. The glow of the screen becomes a barrier, a silent wall between us and our children, effectively stealing the precious moments of uninterrupted connection. We create a paradox: physically close but emotionally distant, creating a void where genuine engagement should be.

Active listening is far more than just hearing the words our children speak. It's about truly hearing them – understanding their unspoken emotions, their underlying anxieties, their hopes and dreams. It's about seeing the world from their perspective, acknowledging their feelings, even when they are difficult or uncomfortable. This involves setting aside our own agendas, our own preoccupations, and focusing entirely on our child in that moment. It's about demonstrating empathy, that deep understanding and compassion that allows us to connect with another human being on a profound level.

Undivided attention is a precious gift, one that our children crave and deeply need. It's about giving them the space to express themselves without interruption, to share their thoughts and feelings without judgment. It's about putting down our phones, turning off the television, and making eye contact, sending a clear message that they are seen, heard, and valued. In these moments of focused attention, we communicate not only our love, but also our respect for their individuality and their inner world.

The power of empathy in building connection cannot be overstated. When children feel truly understood, they are more likely to open up, to share their vulnerabilities, and to trust in the safety of our loving embrace. Empathy involves actively trying to understand their emotions from their point of view, acknowledging the validity of their feelings, and offering support without judgment. It's about creating a safe space where they can explore their emotions without fear of reprimand or ridicule.

Consider the impact of our own emotional state. When we are stressed, overwhelmed, or emotionally depleted, it's difficult to connect with our children in a meaningful way. Our own anxieties and frustrations can subtly permeate the family atmosphere, creating an environment of tension and apprehension. This creates a ripple effect, affecting our children's emotional well-being and damaging the delicate threads of our relationship. It's crucial to prioritize our own mental and emotional health, seeking support when needed, to ensure that we can be fully present for our children.

The importance of shared experiences cannot be overemphasized. The mundane rituals of everyday life—family dinners, bedtime stories, walks in the park—offer invaluable opportunities for connection. These moments provide a space for shared laughter, conversation, and the creation of lasting memories. They aren't just fleeting moments in time; they are the building blocks of a strong and enduring bond. Engage with your children fully in the present. Ask about their day; listen intently to their answers; show genuine interest in their passions. It's the simple acts of engagement that create powerful bonds and nurture the parent-child connection.

The erosion of connection is a gradual process, and its effects may not be immediately apparent. The subtle shifts in behavior – withdrawal, defiance, emotional outbursts – are often dismissed as temporary phases, or attributed to external factors. However, these are often signals of a deeper issue, a disconnect that needs to be addressed before it takes root and blossoms into more serious behavioral or emotional problems. Early intervention is key. Pay attention to the small things, the subtle changes in your child's mood or behavior. These are often the earliest indicators of a weakening connection.

This isn't about perfection; no parent is perfect. It's about making a conscious effort, day in and day out, to nurture the connection with our children. It's about acknowledging our shortcomings, our own vulnerabilities, and recognizing that parenting is a journey, not a destination. We will make
mistakes, we will stumble, but the crucial element is our commitment to repairing the cracks, to rebuilding the bridge of connection, to fostering a loving and supportive relationship that will sustain our children throughout their lives. It's about actively choosing connection over distraction, presence over proximity, and empathy over indifference. This conscious choice to connect profoundly impacts our children's lives, molding their personalities and setting the stage for their futures. The seemingly small moments of connection—a shared hug, a whispered secret, a genuine smile—these are the powerful tools that we can wield to build a strong and enduring connection with our children, and heal the unseen fractures that threaten to undermine their well-being. The investment in connection is the most valuable investment we can make.

Behavioral Red Flags

Aggression, a seemingly straightforward behavioral issue, often masks deeper anxieties and frustrations stemming from inconsistent parenting or a lack of emotional support. A child consistently resorting to physical or verbal aggression might be struggling to communicate unmet needs, feeling unheard, or experiencing overwhelming emotions they lack the skills to process. Consider the scenario of a child who's constantly scolded for minor infractions but receives little positive reinforcement. This creates a sense of insecurity and resentment, potentially manifesting as aggression towards siblings, parents, or peers. The aggression isn't simply bad behavior; it's a cry for help, a desperate attempt to gain attention or control in a world feeling chaotic and unpredictable. Underlying this aggression might be a fear of abandonment, a feeling of powerlessness, or even an underlying trauma that hasn't been addressed. Identifying the root cause is crucial; simply punishing the aggression without addressing the underlying emotional turmoil will likely only exacerbate the problem. This requires attentive observation, open communication, and potentially professional help to understand and address the underlying issues.

Anxiety in children can manifest in various ways, from excessive worry and fear to physical symptoms like stomach aches or difficulty sleeping. Overly permissive parenting, where children are rarely faced with consequences for their actions, can ironically create a breeding ground for anxiety. Without clear boundaries and expectations, children develop a sense of insecurity and uncertainty about the world around them. They may fear disappointing their parents or lack the confidence to navigate challenges independently. Consider a child constantly seeking reassurance from their parents, unable to handle even minor setbacks without significant parental intervention. This constant reliance stems from a lack of trust in their own abilities, fostering a dependency that hinders their emotional growth and contributes to heightened anxiety. Conversely, excessively controlling parenting can also trigger anxiety. Children subjected to constant criticism and high expectations may fear failure and feel unable to meet their parents' demands, leading to debilitating performance anxiety. This manifests not just in academic settings but also in social interactions and everyday life. Identifying the specific parenting style contributing to the anxiety is crucial for effective intervention.

Depression in children, often overlooked or misdiagnosed, presents a serious concern. Symptoms such as persistent sadness, loss of interest in activities, changes in sleep or appetite, and social withdrawal can indicate underlying depression. Children from homes lacking consistent emotional support and nurturing may be more vulnerable to depression. For example, a child consistently exposed to parental conflict or neglect might internalize these negative experiences, leading to low self-esteem and feelings of hopelessness. The delegation of parenting responsibilities to technology, discussed in the previous chapter, can also significantly contribute to a child's depression. The lack of face-to-face interaction and genuine connection can leave a child feeling isolated and emotionally unsupported,

increasing their vulnerability to depression. Moreover, excessive screen time can negatively impact sleep patterns, further exacerbating depressive symptoms. The constant comparison to idealized online personas also contributes to low self-esteem and feelings of inadequacy, amplifying feelings of sadness and isolation. It's vital for parents to recognize these subtle signs and seek professional help, avoiding the temptation to dismiss the child's emotions as simply "a phase."

Poor academic performance often serves as a significant red flag, signaling underlying issues beyond simple laziness or lack of intelligence. A child struggling academically might be grappling with anxiety related to performance pressure, or dealing with learning disabilities that haven't been identified and addressed. The absence of a supportive and encouraging learning environment at home can severely impede a child's academic progress. For instance, a home dominated by constant conflict or parental neglect creates a distracting and emotionally unstable environment, making it difficult for a child to focus on studies. Lack of parental involvement in a child's education, whether through neglecting homework assistance or failing to engage with teachers, contributes to a sense of disengagement and decreased motivation. Further, the excessive use of technology, especially during homework time, can be distracting and detrimental to concentration. The constant barrage of notifications and instant gratification offered by screens make it hard to focus on academic tasks that require sustained attention and effort. Parents must recognize that poor academic performance isn't solely a reflection of the child's capabilities but often reflects the overall quality of the home environment and the level of parental support provided.

Beyond these major behavioral indicators, there are a host of subtler signs demanding parental attention. Consider changes in eating habits – excessive eating or complete loss of appetite – which may signal underlying emotional distress. Sleep disturbances, such as insomnia or excessive sleeping, often mirror anxieties or depression. Changes in social interactions, such as increased withdrawal or aggression towards peers, can be indicative of deeper social-emotional challenges. A sudden drop in self-esteem, manifested through negative self-talk or an unwillingness to participate in activities previously enjoyed, should raise a red flag.

Physical complaints without a clear medical cause often deserve closer scrutiny, particularly if these complaints coincide with other behavioral or emotional changes. These symptoms are not isolated incidents but interconnected manifestations of a larger underlying issue that requires careful assessment. Dismissing these signs as insignificant can delay critical intervention and allow the "hidden crack" to widen, impacting the child's well-being significantly.

It's crucial to remember that these behavioral red flags are interconnected. For example, a child experiencing anxiety might exhibit aggression as a coping mechanism, while a child struggling with depression may withdraw socially and show poor academic performance. The interplay of these symptoms highlights the complexity of understanding a child's behavioral issues. Parents should avoid focusing solely on one specific behavior and instead consider the holistic picture. A pattern of seemingly unrelated behaviors –such as aggression towards siblings, difficulty sleeping, and a drop in grades – may indicate a deeper underlying. This requires systematic observation, careful documentation of concerning behaviors, and ideally, professional assessment. The identification of a single red flag should prompt a deeper investigation into the child's overall well-being.

The path to understanding and addressing these issues isn't always linear. There might be instances where initial interventions prove ineffective, requiring a reassessment of the approach. Parental self-reflection plays a crucial role in this process. Honesty in recognizing personal limitations and willingness to seek external support are paramount. The tendency to blame the child for difficult behaviors must be replaced with a compassionate effort to understand the root causes, acknowledging that flawed parenting styles, societal pressures, and unforeseen circumstances all play a part. Parents must remember that seeking professional help is not a sign of failure but rather a testament to their commitment to their child's well-being. Professional guidance offers invaluable support in navigating complex behavioral issues, providing a framework for effective intervention and empowering parents with the skills and strategies to foster healthier relationships with their children. This includes understanding different therapeutic approaches, learning effective communication strategies, and developing coping mechanisms for both the child and the parent. The journey may be challenging, but the investment in understanding and addressing these warning signs ultimately protects and nurtures the child's growth, paving the way for a brighter future.

Social and Emotional Deficits

The absence of consistent guidance and emotional support leaves a gaping hole in a child's development, profoundly impacting their ability to navigate the complexities of social interactions and emotional regulation. This deficit manifests in various ways, often subtle at first, but gradually escalating into significant challenges as the child grows. The foundation of healthy relationships is built upon a bedrock of secure attachment, empathy, and effective communication—skills that are nurtured through consistent, responsive parenting. When this nurturing is absent or deficient, the resulting cracks in the foundation can lead to a cascade of social and emotional difficulties.

One of the most prevalent consequences is the struggle to form and maintain healthy relationships. Children who lack emotional intelligence, often due to a lack of parental modeling or guidance, may struggle to understand and respond appropriately to the emotions of others. They might misinterpret social cues, leading to misunderstandings and conflict. Imagine a child who consistently interrupts conversations, oblivious to the frustration it causes. This isn't necessarily malice; it could be a lack of awareness of social norms and emotional boundaries, a deficit stemming from a lack of consistent guidance and positive reinforcement of appropriate social behaviors. Similarly, a child might

struggle to read nonverbal cues, failing to recognize when a peer is upset or feeling excluded. This inability to empathize can lead to social isolation, as peers find it difficult to connect with someone who doesn't seem to understand their feelings. The difficulties extend beyond simple misunderstandings.

Children lacking emotional support may develop insecure attachment styles, characterized by anxiety, clinginess, or avoidance in relationships. A child who experiences inconsistent parental responses to their needs might develop an anxious attachment, constantly seeking reassurance and validation, fearing abandonment or rejection. Conversely, a child who's consistently ignored or dismissed might develop an avoidant attachment, pushing people away and suppressing their emotional needs to avoid potential hurt.

These insecure attachments can significantly impact their future relationships, impacting romantic partnerships, friendships, and even professional collaborations. They might struggle to trust others, fearing intimacy or vulnerability. They may enter relationships with a heightened sense of insecurity, constantly seeking external validation or displaying controlling behaviors to compensate for their underlying anxieties.

Beyond relational challenges, emotional deficits can manifest as difficulties in emotional regulation. A child who lacks the skills to manage their emotions might exhibit extreme reactions to minor setbacks or frustrations.

Tantrums, outbursts of anger, or persistent sadness can become common occurrences. This isn't simply "bad behavior"; it's a reflection of an underdeveloped capacity to process and regulate emotions. This inability stems from a lack of parental modeling and guidance in healthy emotional expression. Parents who consistently dismiss or minimize a child's feelings are inadvertently teaching them that their emotions are invalid or unimportant. This can lead to emotional suppression, where the child learns to bottle up their feelings, eventually leading to emotional explosions or chronic anxiety.

The lack of emotional vocabulary and understanding further complicates matters. If a child hasn't been taught to name and articulate their emotions, they might struggle to communicate their needs and feelings effectively. They might resort to acting out or withdrawing, as these become their default mechanisms for expressing internal distress. Imagine a child who feels overwhelmed by anxiety before a test but lacks the language to express this fear. They might instead exhibit disruptive behavior in class or withdraw completely, their distress remaining unspoken and unaddressed.

Academic struggles often accompany social and emotional deficits. A child battling anxiety or depression might struggle to concentrate in class, leading to poor academic performance. The constant worry or sadness drains their energy and focus, making it difficult to engage with learning. Furthermore, the lack of emotional regulation can interfere with their ability to manage frustration or setbacks in their studies. They might give up easily when faced with challenges or exhibit disruptive behavior when they feel overwhelmed. A child's emotional well-being directly impacts their cognitive performance. A supportive and understanding environment, where emotional needs are met and emotional intelligence is fostered, creates a fertile ground for academic success.

The ripple effects of these deficits extend far beyond childhood. Adults who struggled with emotional regulation and social skills as children may continue to experience difficulties in their relationships and careers. They might struggle with intimacy, trust, and conflict resolution. They may find it difficult to manage stress and navigate professional challenges. The patterns established in childhood can create a self-perpetuating cycle of difficulties, unless actively addressed and overcome.

Consider the long-term implications: A young adult struggling to maintain healthy relationships, perpetually plagued by insecurity and anxiety, might find themselves in unhealthy or abusive relationships. A professional grappling with difficulty managing stress and emotions might find their career trajectory hampered by anxiety, burnout, and interpersonal conflicts. The consequences of unchecked emotional and social deficits can be far-reaching and deeply impactful, highlighting the critical importance of early intervention and parental involvement.

The solution isn't simply about providing more structured activities or enrolling a child in social skills training, although these can be beneficial components of a comprehensive approach. It's about fostering a loving and supportive environment where a child feels safe to express their emotions, both positive and negative, without fear of judgment or dismissal. This necessitates conscious parenting—a mindful and deliberate approach to raising children that prioritizes emotional connection, empathetic understanding, and consistent guidance.

Parents need to cultivate a deep understanding of their children's emotional landscape. This involves actively listening to their concerns, validating their feelings, and teaching them healthy coping mechanisms. It requires patience, empathy, and a willingness to engage in open and honest communication. It means setting clear and consistent boundaries, providing a sense of security and predictability in their lives. It also involves modeling healthy emotional regulation—showing children how to manage their emotions in constructive ways, rather than resorting to outbursts or suppression.

Furthermore, parents need to actively teach children emotional literacy. This involves expanding their emotional vocabulary, helping them identify and name different emotions, both in themselves and in others. It involves discussing emotional situations, providing context and understanding, and helping children develop strategies for managing difficult emotions. Simple exercises, like reading books about emotions or engaging in role-playing scenarios, can be immensely helpful.

Recognizing the social and emotional deficits arising from inadequate parental guidance is not about assigning blame; it's about understanding the complex interplay of factors that contribute to a child's development. It's about recognizing the significant impact of parental behavior and creating a foundation for healthier emotional and social development.

It's a call to action for parents to prioritize genuine connection, empathetic understanding, and conscious parenting, recognizing that the investment in their children's emotional well-being is an investment in their future happiness and success. This journey requires self-reflection, a willingness to seek help when needed, and an unwavering commitment to fostering a nurturing and supportive environment for their children to thrive. The long-term rewards of such an investment are immeasurable.

Academic Struggles

The cracks in a child's foundation, subtly revealed through emotional and social struggles, often manifest in another crucial area: academics. While a child's intelligence and inherent aptitude play a role, their academic performance is surprisingly intertwined with the quality of their upbringing and the parenting style they experience. A lack of consistent boundaries, insufficient emotional support, and an over-reliance on technology can significantly undermine a child's ability to thrive academically. This isn't about blaming parents; it's about understanding the complex relationship between parenting and a child's academic success.

One of the most significant ways parenting impacts academics is through its influence on motivation. Children who feel loved, understood, and supported are more likely to be intrinsically motivated. They approach learning with a sense of curiosity and a desire to master new skills, not simply to earn good grades. Conversely, children raised in environments lacking consistent support and emotional connection may develop a sense of inadequacy or helplessness. They may see academic pursuits as a source of stress and anxiety rather than an opportunity for growth.

This lack of intrinsic motivation often leads to procrastination, avoidance, and ultimately, poor academic performance. Imagine a child constantly berated for poor grades, never praised for effort, perpetually feeling judged instead of encouraged. Their inherent desire to learn is likely to be crushed under the weight of constant negativity.

Furthermore, a child's ability to focus and concentrate directly correlates with the stability and structure of their home environment. Children who experience chaos, inconsistency, or frequent parental conflict often struggle to concentrate in school. Their minds are preoccupied with anxieties about their home life, making it difficult to engage in learning. A home that provides a calm, organized, and predictable environment, on the other hand, fosters a sense of security that allows children to focus their attention on their studies. Think of it like a plant – a plant needs consistent sunlight, water, and nutrients to thrive. Similarly, a child needs a stable environment to grow and flourish academically.

Study habits, too, are profoundly influenced by parenting styles. Parents who actively participate in their children's education, helping them develop organizational skills, time-management techniques, and effective study strategies, are providing their children with a significant advantage. This involvement goes beyond simply checking homework; it includes creating a dedicated study space, establishing
consistent study routines, and fostering a positive attitude towards learning. In contrast, children from homes where parental involvement is minimal or characterized by disinterest are often left to fend for themselves academically, developing poor study habits and struggling to keep pace with their peers. A child left to navigate the complex world of assignments, tests, and deadlines without guidance is akin to a sailor navigating a storm without a compass.

The pervasive influence of technology further complicates the picture. Excessive screen time, particularly in the absence of appropriate parental oversight, significantly impacts a child's ability to focus, regulate emotions, and develop essential learning skills. The constant stimulation of screens can lead to attention deficits, making it difficult for children to concentrate on tasks requiring sustained
attention, such as reading, writing, or problem-solving.

Furthermore, excessive screen time often comes at the expense of other activities crucial for academic success, such as sleep, exercise, and social interaction. The impact on sleep alone is substantial; sleep deprivation directly affects cognitive function, memory, and overall academic performance. It's a vicious cycle; poor sleep leads to poor concentration, leading to poor academic performance, leading to further stress and sleep deprivation.

The delegation of child-rearing responsibilities to technology and social media, a common occurrence in today's fast-paced world, further exacerbates these issues. When parents rely on screens to occupy their children, they miss opportunities to engage in meaningful interactions, build strong relationships, and provide the emotional support necessary for academic success. This reliance on technology creates a sense of detachment, hindering the development of essential communication and social skills that contribute significantly to a child's ability to learn effectively both individually and collaboratively. A child who struggles to interact effectively with teachers and peers will inevitably face greater academic challenges.

Moreover, the prioritization of financial provision over genuine connection and guidance can also lead to academic struggles. While financial security is essential, it cannot replace the emotional support and mentorship that are crucial for a child's academic success. Children who feel loved, valued, and understood are more likely to persevere through challenges, develop resilience, and achieve their academic potential. In contrast, children who feel neglected or emotionally unsupported may lack the motivation and self-esteem to overcome academic hurdles. The relentless pursuit of financial success at the expense of parental presence and involvement creates a void in a child's life that is difficult to fill, often manifesting as academic underachievement.

It's crucial to understand that addressing academic struggles requires a holistic approach. It's not just about improving study habits or boosting test scores; it's about addressing the underlying emotional, social, and relational factors that contribute to a child's academic performance. This requires parents to reflect on their parenting styles, to identify areas where they can provide more support and guidance, and to cultivate a nurturing and supportive environment conducive to learning.

Practical strategies for parents include creating a dedicated study space, establishing a consistent study routine, fostering open communication about schoolwork, providing assistance with organizational skills, and celebrating effort and progress rather than focusing solely on grades. Engaging children in active learning, encouraging curiosity, and providing opportunities for exploration and discovery are equally important. Furthermore, limiting screen time, promoting healthy sleep habits, and fostering healthy relationships with peers and teachers are crucial for supporting a child's academic journey. Open communication with teachers is also paramount; understanding a child's strengths and weaknesses from the teacher's perspective provides invaluable insight for parents.

Ultimately, addressing the academic struggles stemming from the cracks in a child's foundation requires a shift in parental mindset. It's about moving away from a performance-driven approach to education and embracing a more holistic view that prioritizes a child's emotional well-being and overall development. Parents must actively participate in their children's education, providing support, guidance, and encouragement at every stage of their journey.

It's about creating a loving and supportive environment where children feel safe to learn, grow, and reach their full potential. The investment in their children's academic success is an investment in their future, an investment that yields immeasurable rewards. The journey requires patience, understanding, and a commitment to fostering a strong, supportive, and loving family dynamic. Remember, the goal isn't just to achieve high grades; it's to nurture a lifelong love of learning and a well-rounded, confident, and resilient individual.

THREE
PHYSICAL HEALTH INDICATORS

The emotional and academic struggles we've explored are often mirrored, and sometimes even triggered, by disturbances in a child's physical health. While genetics play a role, the environment a child grows up in, shaped significantly by parenting styles, exerts a profound influence on their physical well-being. This isn't a simple cause-and-effect relationship; it's a complex interplay of factors, where a 'hidden crack' in the foundation can manifest as physical symptoms. One of the most common indicators is sleep disruption. A child consistently struggling with insomnia, waking frequently during the night, or experiencing excessive daytime sleepiness might not just be battling a simple bedtime routine issue; it could be a reflection of underlying anxieties, stress, or emotional turmoil stemming from their home environment. A parent's constant arguing, an overbearing disciplinary style, or a general lack of security and stability in the home can translate into a child's inability to relax and find restful sleep. This isn't about blaming parents for their child's sleep problems; it's about recognizing that a child's sleep is a window into their inner world, a reflection of their emotional and psychological state.

Consider a child who suddenly develops an aversion to food or exhibits erratic eating habits. This might manifest as extreme pickiness, refusing entire food groups, or, conversely, excessive eating and a struggle with weight management. These behaviors rarely appear in isolation.

They often accompany emotional distress. A child feeling neglected, unloved, or constantly criticized might find solace or control in manipulating their food intake. An eating disorder isn't simply a physical ailment; it's often a cry for help, a desperate attempt to regain a sense of control in a chaotic or emotionally turbulent environment. The lack of consistent boundaries and the failure to provide a secure attachment figure can contribute to this deeply rooted issue.

Parents, often unaware of the emotional roots of the problem, might focus on the physical symptoms, overlooking the underlying emotional distress, potentially exacerbating the issue. It is vital to remember that addressing the eating disorder requires addressing the emotional wounds that lie beneath the surface, creating a supportive and understanding environment where the child feels safe and valued.

Beyond sleep disturbances and eating disorders, physical health indicators can also manifest in other ways.Headaches, stomachaches, and other somatic complaints often accompany anxiety and stress. A child consistently complaining of physical ailments without any clear medical explanation could be signaling that something is wrong in their emotional world. These are not imagined illnesses; they are real physical manifestations of emotional distress. The pressure to excel academically, the constant criticism, or the lack of emotional support at home can manifest as chronic physical symptoms, leaving the child trapped in a cycle of pain and discomfort. In such cases, it's crucial to look beyond the immediate physical symptoms and delve into the underlying emotional turmoil that might be driving them. A child might be struggling to articulate their feelings,resorting to physical manifestations as a way of communicating their inner distress. A collaborative approach between parents, doctors, and possibly therapists is often essential in addressing these complex issues.

The constant pressure to conform, to perform, and to achieve can take a significant toll on a child's physical health. The relentless pursuit of perfection, often fueled by parental expectations, can lead to chronic stress, anxiety, and even depression. This pressure can translate into a variety of physical manifestations, including weakened immunity, increased susceptibility to illness, and various other health problems. The impact is profound and far-reaching, potentially affecting the child's overall development and well-being. Children under immense pressure might experience physical symptoms like weakened immunity, resulting in frequent illnesses. The constant state of anxiety and stress can disrupt the body's natural ability to fight off infections, leaving them vulnerable to various health issues.

Furthermore, the over-reliance on technology, a common feature in today's parenting landscape, also contributes to several physical health concerns. Excessive screen time has been linked to a variety of physical problems, including eye strain, sleep disturbances, obesity, and poor posture.

Children spending hours glued to screens often neglect physical activity, resulting in a sedentary lifestyle and an increased risk of developing obesity and related health problems. The blue light emitted from electronic devices can disrupt the body's natural sleep-wake cycle, leading to sleep deprivation and its associated physical and mental health consequences. Poor posture due to prolonged screen time can lead to long-term musculoskeletal issues, affecting the child's physical well-being in the years to come. This isn't about demonizing technology; it's about mindful usage and establishing healthy boundaries to prevent these detrimental physical effects.

Moreover, the lack of proper nutrition, often a consequence of busy lifestyles and parental neglect, significantly impacts a child's physical health. Parents overwhelmed with work and other commitments might resort to convenience foods, neglecting the importance of balanced nutrition for their children's growth and development. This lack of nutritional sustenance can lead to weakened immunity, stunted growth, and various other health problems. The nutritional deficiencies can manifest in different ways, from fatigue and lethargy to impaired cognitive function and an increased susceptibility to illness. A child's diet plays a critical role in their overall health and well-being, influencing not only their physical development but also their cognitive abilities and emotional stability. Parents need to prioritize providing their children with nutritious meals and educating them about healthy eating habits to ensure their physical well-being.

Another often-overlooked aspect is the impact of parental stress on a child's physical health. When parents are chronically stressed, their children often absorb that stress, leading to various physical and emotional problems.

Children are incredibly perceptive and sensitive to their parents' emotional state. Parental stress can manifest in different ways, from increased irritability and a lack of patience to neglect and inconsistent discipline. This can create an environment where the child feels insecure, anxious, and stressed, leading to various physical manifestations of that stress. It's crucial for parents to recognize their own stress levels and to actively seek ways to manage them to create a more stable and supportive environment for their children.

The physical manifestations of a 'hidden crack' are often subtle, easily dismissed as temporary ailments or minor inconveniences. However, these signs can be vital clues to deeper underlying issues that require attention and intervention. It's not just about treating the physical symptoms; it's about understanding the root causes, addressing the underlying emotional and psychological issues, and fostering a nurturing environment that promotes physical and emotional well-being. This requires a holistic approach, involving open communication, collaboration with healthcare professionals, and a genuine commitment to understanding and meeting the child's needs. The goal is not simply to eliminate the physical symptoms; it's to create a healthier, more supportive family dynamic that fosters the child's overall well-being, preventing long-term consequences. Remember, a child's physical health is intimately connected to their emotional and psychological well-being, and addressing the 'hidden crack' requires a comprehensive and multifaceted approach. The path to healing is not always easy, but it's a journey worth taking, leading to a stronger, healthier, and more resilient child.

Early Intervention is Key

The earlier we address the cracks appearing in a child's foundation, the easier it is to mend them. Delaying intervention, hoping things will magically improve, is a dangerous gamble. The longer these issues persist, the deeper they become embedded, potentially leading to entrenched behavioral patterns, academic struggles, and lasting emotional scars. Think of it like a small fissure in a dam; initially, it might seem insignificant, but if left unchecked, the water pressure will inevitably cause a catastrophic breach. Similarly, a seemingly minor behavioral issue in childhood can escalate into significant problems in adolescence and adulthood if not addressed promptly.

This isn't about instantly labeling a child with a disorder or pathologizing normal childhood behavior. It's about recognizing subtle shifts in behavior, changes in mood, or persistent difficulties that might signal underlying issues.

Perhaps your once-outgoing child has become withdrawn, spending increasingly more time alone. Maybe your cheerful, cooperative child is now defiant and irritable, consistently pushing boundaries. Or perhaps your previously high-achieving student is struggling to keep up with their schoolwork, demonstrating a sudden drop in grades. These changes, while seemingly small on their own, can be significant when viewed collectively. They might be subtle whispers of a larger problem waiting to be unearthed.

The process of seeking professional help can feel daunting. Many parents worry about the stigma associated with seeking therapy or counseling, fearing judgment from others.

However, this is a misguided fear. Seeking help for your child is a sign of strength, not weakness. It demonstrates a commitment to your child's well-being and a proactive approach to addressing potential challenges. Remember, just as you wouldn't hesitate to consult a doctor for a physical ailment, addressing emotional and behavioral concerns requires the expertise of a qualified professional.

Choosing the right professional is crucial. There's a wide range of specialists who can assist, each with their own area of expertise. Child psychologists specialize in the mental and emotional development of children, offering insights into behavioral issues, learning disabilities, and emotional regulation. Pediatricians often act as a first point of contact, able to identify physical issues that might be contributing to behavioral problems. Educational psychologists work with schools to identify learning difficulties and develop individualized education plans. Therapists, such as family therapists or play therapists, can work with the entire family to address relational dynamics and improve communication. The best choice will depend on your child's specific needs and the nature of the challenges you're facing.

When contacting a professional, be prepared to provide a detailed account of your concerns. This includes describing the specific behaviors you're witnessing, when they started, their frequency, and any potential triggers or contributing factors. Don't shy away from sharing personal information about your family dynamics, parenting styles, and any stressors you might be facing. The more comprehensive the information you provide, the better equipped the professional is to understand the situation and develop an effective intervention plan.

The initial consultation usually involves a thorough assessment of your child. This might involve interviews with you, your child (depending on their age and maturity), and possibly other family members. There may be standardized

tests to assess cognitive abilities, learning styles, and emotional development. The professional will use this information to create a clear picture of your child's strengths and weaknesses, identifying potential areas for intervention.

Once the assessment is complete, the professional will likely develop a treatment plan tailored to your child's specific needs. This plan might involve individual therapy, family therapy, behavioral interventions, or a combination of approaches. The frequency and duration of sessions will depend on the severity of the issues and the child's progress.

Remember, this is a collaborative process. Open communication with the professional is crucial. Don't hesitate to express any concerns or questions you have throughout the treatment process.

The goal of intervention isn't to "fix" the child; it's to empower them with the skills and strategies needed to navigate challenges and thrive. It's about building resilience, fostering emotional intelligence, and improving their ability to cope with stress. This includes equipping parents with the tools and knowledge to create a supportive and nurturing environment at home, fostering open communication and understanding.

Early intervention often involves a multifaceted approach, incorporating adjustments in the home environment, school strategies, and therapeutic interventions. It's crucial that all key figures in the child's life—parents, teachers, therapists—work together in a collaborative manner. This integrated approach greatly enhances the chances of positive outcomes. A consistent, supportive network significantly contributes to a child's healing journey.

Consider the case of eight-year-old Lily. Her parents noticed a gradual change in her behavior – she became increasingly withdrawn, losing interest in activities she once loved. Her grades started to slip, and she would frequently complain of headaches and stomachaches. Initially, her parents attributed these to stress at school or a minor illness. However, when the symptoms persisted, they sought professional help.

Through therapy, it was discovered that Lily was experiencing significant anxiety related to a bullying incident at school. Her therapist used play therapy to help her process her emotions, develop coping mechanisms, and regain her confidence. Her parents, guided by the therapist, implemented strategies to improve communication and build a stronger support system at home. Through this combined effort, Lily's anxiety gradually subsided, her grades improved, and she regained her zest for life.

Another example is ten-year-old Tom, who was displaying increasingly disruptive behavior at school. He would constantly interrupt class, argue with teachers, and refuse to follow instructions. His parents, initially frustrated, tried different disciplinary techniques, none of which seemed to work. They finally consulted a child psychologist who identified underlying ADHD (attention deficit hyperactivity disorder). With a proper diagnosis and the implementation of behavioral strategies, both at home and in school, Tom's behavior improved significantly. This demonstrates the power of early intervention – addressing the root cause of the behavior rather than simply trying to suppress the symptoms.

Early intervention isn't always a quick fix. It requires patience, persistence, and a willingness to adapt strategies as needed. There might be setbacks along the way, but consistent effort, coupled with professional guidance, usually leads to positive outcomes. The earlier you seek help, the better chance your child has to develop healthy coping mechanisms and build a strong foundation for their future.

Remember, you're not alone in this journey. Seeking support is a sign of strength, and it's a crucial step towards fostering a healthier and happier future for your child. The goal is not just to eliminate immediate problems but to equip your child with the tools to navigate life's inevitable challenges with resilience and confidence. And that, in the long run, is the greatest gift you can give them.

The impact of early intervention cannot be overstated. It's about preventing small problems from escalating into significant long-term issues. By addressing challenges early, we can prevent the development of more severe behavioral, emotional, or academic problems later on. This proactive approach not only helps the child but also alleviates significant stress for the entire family, preventing the development of chronic family conflict and emotional strain.

Early intervention offers the best chance for positive outcomes and fosters healthier, more resilient children and families. It allows for the development of effective coping mechanisms before problems become entrenched, reducing the need for more intensive and prolonged interventions later in life.

The road to a healthier, more balanced family life isn't always smooth. It involves acknowledging challenges, seeking guidance, and embracing a journey of growth and understanding. It requires open communication, empathy, and a commitment to creating a nurturing and supportive environment. By recognizing the warning signs and seeking help early, you're not just addressing current issues; you're investing in your child's future well-being, laying a strong foundation for a fulfilling and successful life. And that, ultimately, is the most valuable gift any parent can give.

Remember, seeking help isn't a sign of failure; it's a courageous step towards building a brighter future for your child. Don't hesitate to reach out; the resources and support are available. The journey towards a healthier family dynamic is one worth taking. It's a journey of learning, adapting, and growing together, leading to a stronger, more resilient, and ultimately, happier family. The effort you invest will undoubtedly pay off, enriching the lives of both your child and your entire family. And that's a legacy worth building.

FOUR
MINDFUL PARENTING TECHNIQUES

The journey of parenthood is rarely a smooth, predictable path. It's a winding road filled with unexpected detours, steep inclines, and exhilarating stretches of open highway. We've explored the potential pitfalls – the hidden cracks that can form in the foundation of a parent-child relationship, stemming from the pressures of modern life and well-intentioned but misguided approaches to raising children.

Now, let's focus on building a stronger, more resilient foundation: a foundation built on mindful parenting. Mindful parenting isn't about achieving perfection; it's about cultivating a conscious awareness of your interactions with your child. It's about being present, truly present, in those moments that shape their lives, rather than drifting through them distracted by the endless demands of work, technology, or even our own inner anxieties. It's about recognizing that your child isn't just a miniature adult waiting to be molded, but a unique individual with their own thoughts, feelings, and needs.

Active listening is the cornerstone of mindful parenting. It's more than just hearing your child's words; it's about understanding their underlying emotions. Imagine your teenager slumped on the couch, headphones on, barely acknowledging your presence. Instead of launching into a lecture about their responsibilities, try this: sit beside them, maintain eye contact, and simply say, "Hey, you seem a little down. Anything you want to talk about?" This simple act of acknowledgement can open the door to deeper communication. It demonstrates that you see them, hear them, and care about their inner world. Don't interrupt; let them express themselves fully, even if what they say seems trivial or inconsequential to you. Your undivided attention is the most valuable gift you can offer.

Empathy, the ability to understand and share the feelings of another, is equally crucial. When your child is upset, angry, or frustrated, try to step into their shoes. What might be causing their distress? What are they feeling beneath the surface? Even if you don't fully agree with their perspective, acknowledge their emotions. Say things like, "That sounds really frustrating," or, "I can see you're feeling hurt." This validation helps your child feel understood and less alone in their experience.

Setting healthy boundaries is another vital component of mindful parenting. Boundaries aren't about control; they're about providing structure and safety. They help children understand expectations, develop self-discipline, and learn to navigate the world responsibly. These boundaries should be clear, consistent, and age-appropriate. A five-year-old needs different boundaries than a fifteen-year-old. Explain the reasons behind the boundaries, emphasizing the importance of their safety and well-being. When consequences are necessary, ensure they are fair and directly related to the child's actions. Avoid using punishment as a means of emotional control or retaliation.

Mindful parenting isn't just about your interactions with your child; it's also about cultivating self-awareness. Take time for self-reflection. How are your own emotions affecting your parenting style? Are you consistently reacting rather than responding to your child's behavior? Are you consistently prioritizing your own needs over your child's needs? If so, it's time to pause, take a deep breath, and approach the situation with a fresh perspective. Mindfulness practices, such as meditation or deep breathing exercises, can be invaluable tools for managing stress and improving your emotional regulation.

Consider the scenario of a parent consistently stressed from work. They come home to a messy room and a child glued to a screen. Instead of reacting with anger, a mindful parent might take a moment to calm themselves, possibly engaging in a brief mindfulness exercise. Then, instead of yelling, they might calmly address the situation, asking the child to help clean up and suggesting an alternative activity that
encourages engagement and connection. This small change reflects a significant shift from reaction to response.

Another crucial aspect is fostering a sense of security and trust. Children thrive in environments where they feel safe, loved, and accepted, unconditionally. This doesn't mean condoning bad behavior, but it does mean offering unwavering support and empathy, even when your child makes mistakes. Let them know that your love is not contingent upon their actions or achievements. Create a safe space where they can express their vulnerabilities without fear of judgment. This might be a quiet corner of their room, a special time set aside for one-on-one conversation, or even a family game night where everyone feels comfortable sharing their thoughts and feelings. Effective communication is key to building this trust.

Remember the importance of active listening. But also, learn to communicate your own feelings and needs clearly and respectfully. Use "I" statements to express yourself without blaming or accusing. For example, instead of saying, "You always leave your clothes on the floor," try, "I feel frustrated when I see clothes on the floor because it makes the room messy." Tailor your communication style to your child's age and developmental stage. A toddler will respond differently than a teenager.

Building a strong parent-child bond requires consistent effort and a willingness to adapt your approach as your child grows and changes. Remember that this isn't a race; it's a journey, a lifelong relationship that will evolve and deepen over time.

The goal isn't perfection but progress. Celebrate small victories, learn from mistakes, and embrace the imperfections that make your family unique.

Beyond active listening, empathy, and healthy boundaries, remember the power of shared experiences. Engage in activities you both enjoy, whether it's baking cookies,
playing a board game, reading together, or simply enjoying a quiet evening at home. These shared moments create lasting memories and strengthen your bond. Unplug from
technology and be fully present in those interactions.

Incorporate family rituals and traditions into your daily life. These routines provide a sense of normalcy, predictability, and belonging. They create opportunities for connection and shared laughter. Whether it's a weekly family dinner, a regular game night, or a yearly vacation, these traditions become anchors of stability and create positive associations with family life.

Mindful parenting necessitates self-care. It's impossible to pour from an empty cup. Parents need time to recharge, de-stress, and nurture their own well-being. Make time for activities that bring you joy and peace, whether it's exercise, reading, spending time in nature, or pursuing a hobby.

Prioritize your physical and mental health so you can be the best parent you can be. Self-care isn't selfish; it's essential for creating a supportive and nurturing family environment.

Remember that taking care of yourself enables you to be more present and engaged with your children.

Finally, remember that you are not alone. Parenting is challenging, and it's perfectly acceptable to seek support when you need it. Connect with other parents, join a support group, or consult with a therapist or counselor if you're struggling. Don't hesitate to ask for help; seeking support is a sign of strength, not weakness.

Mindful parenting is a transformative approach, demanding both introspection and action. It's about making conscious choices to build a stronger, more nurturing relationship with your child, one that is based on mutual respect, empathy, and unconditional love. This, in turn, fosters a secure foundation for your child to navigate the complexities of life, equipping them with the resilience and emotional intelligence to thrive. It's a journey of continuous learning, adaptation, and growth– a journey that, while challenging, is ultimately profoundly rewarding.

The Power of Unconditional Love

Unconditional love isn't a fluffy, feel-good concept; it's the bedrock upon which a healthy parent-child relationship is built. It's the unwavering belief in your child's inherent worth, a belief that remains unshaken regardless of their mistakes, their struggles, or even their defiant acts. It's a love that sees beyond the surface, recognizing the vulnerable, growing human being beneath the sometimes challenging exterior. This isn't about condoning bad behavior; it's about understanding the underlying reasons behind it. It's about separating the action from the child, loving the child fiercely while simultaneously setting healthy boundaries and guiding them towards better choices.

Think of it as a lighthouse in a storm. The storm represents the inevitable challenges your child will face – academic setbacks, social difficulties, emotional turmoil. The lighthouse, unwavering and steadfast, is your unconditional love, offering a beacon of hope and safety in the midst of the tempest. It's not about shielding your child from the storm entirely; that's impossible, and ultimately unhelpful. It's about providing a safe harbor to return to, a place where they know they are unconditionally loved, accepted, and valued, no matter how turbulent the waters may become.

This doesn't mean your love is passive. It's an active force, a constant presence in your child's life. It's in the quiet moments of listening, truly listening, without judgment or interruption. It's in the gentle touch, the reassuring hug, the whispered words of encouragement. It's in the consistent, reliable presence of a loving parent, offering support and guidance, even when your child pushes you away. It's the unwavering belief in their potential, even when they doubt themselves. It's celebrating their small victories with as much enthusiasm as their larger accomplishments.

Many parents mistakenly confuse unconditional love with permissiveness. They believe that showing unconditional love means allowing their child to do whatever they want, without consequences or boundaries. This is a dangerous misconception. Unconditional love does not mean unfettered freedom; it means loving your child enough to guide them, to set limits, and to help them learn from their mistakes. It's about helping them develop self-discipline, responsibility, and empathy.

For example, imagine a child who consistently refuses to do their homework. A parent operating from a place of conditional love might react with anger, punishment, or withdrawal of affection. They might say, "I don't love you when you're disobedient," inadvertently communicating that their love is contingent upon their child's behavior. In contrast, a parent offering unconditional love would still express disappointment, but they would also maintain their love and support. They might say, "Honey, I know this is hard, but I believe in you. Let's work together to figure out a plan to make homework less challenging." They would focus on understanding the root cause – is it a learning disability? Is it a lack of organizational skills? Is it simply avoidance? Once the root is identified, strategies can be implemented to address it, collaboratively.

This approach acknowledges the child's struggle without condoning the behavior. It maintains a connection, strengthening the bond, even amidst conflict. This doesn't mean avoiding consequences; rather, consequences become opportunities for teaching and growth, rather than punitive measures aimed at inflicting pain or withdrawing affection.

The focus is always on the child's well-being and development, fostering self-esteem and resilience. Discipline becomes a tool for guidance, not punishment.

Consider the teenager who makes a significant mistake, perhaps involving drugs or risky behavior. A parent's immediate reaction might be outrage, fear, and disappointment. However, even in such extreme cases, unconditional love remains the compass guiding parental action. The focus shifts from blame and punishment towards understanding, support, and rehabilitation. This doesn't minimize the seriousness of the situation; instead, it acknowledges the complexity of the circumstances and the child's vulnerability. It means seeking professional help, ensuring the child's safety, and working together to navigate the crisis. The message remains consistent: "I love you, but your actions have consequences. We'll face this together."

Unconditional love also extends to accepting your child's individuality. It means celebrating their unique talents, interests, and perspectives, even if they differ from your own. It's about fostering their independence and autonomy, encouraging them to explore their passions and discover their own path in life. It means providing a safe space for them to express their feelings, their fears, and their dreams, without judgment or criticism. This acceptance is crucial in developing a strong sense of self and building resilience against external pressures.

It's important to remember that offering unconditional love doesn't mean you're a pushover. It's about creating a balance between love, guidance, and boundaries. It requires setting clear expectations and enforcing consequences for unacceptable behavior, while simultaneously ensuring your child feels loved, accepted, and supported. It's about acknowledging that children make mistakes and that these mistakes are opportunities for learning and growth.

Building a relationship founded on unconditional love is a lifelong commitment, requiring patience, empathy, and unwavering dedication. It's a journey of continuous learning, adaptation, and growth, with both parents and children continuously evolving and changing. There will be times when you question your own ability to provide this unconditional love, especially during challenging periods.

However, it is precisely during those challenging times that its importance becomes most profound. Think of it as a garden. You nurture your plants, provide water and sunlight, and remove weeds. Sometimes, despite your best efforts, a plant may wilt or die. But you don't stop tending the garden. You learn from what happened, adjust your methods, and continue to cultivate the remaining plants.

Parenting is similar. You'll encounter challenges, setbacks, and moments of frustration. Unconditional love is the fertile soil that enables your child to thrive, even amidst adversity. It's the unwavering commitment to nurturing their growth, regardless of the challenges you face along the way.

This doesn't mean ignoring behavioral issues or failing to intervene when necessary. Unconditional love is not passive; it is an active force, constantly shaping and guiding. It requires setting healthy boundaries and expectations, while simultaneously offering support, encouragement, and empathy. It means celebrating successes and providing comfort during setbacks. It's about helping your child develop into a well-rounded, responsible, and compassionate individual.

The journey of providing unconditional love is ongoing. There will be moments of doubt, moments of frustration, and moments when you question your own capacity for such unwavering affection. These moments are normal. It's vital to remember that this is not a perfect, flawless process. It's a journey of continuous learning, growth, and adaptation for both parents and children. The commitment to unconditional love isn't just about feeling a certain way, it's about actively choosing to love, support, and guide your child, no matter what. It's about creating a foundation of trust and security that allows your child to flourish. This foundation will serve as their steadfast support system, empowering them to

navigate life's inevitable challenges with resilience, compassion, and strength. It's the most precious gift you can give them.

Effective Communication Strategies

Building upon that foundation of unconditional love, we now turn to the crucial skill of effective communication. It's not simply about talking at your child; it's about truly connecting, understanding, and being understood. This is a skill that requires constant practice and adaptation, evolving as your child grows and their communication abilities develop. The way you speak to a toddler differs significantly from how you converse with a teenager, and failing to recognize this difference can lead to misunderstandings and strained relationships.

Effective communication begins with active listening. This isn't passive hearing; it's about genuinely focusing on your child's words, their body language, and the emotions they're conveying. Put down your phone, make eye contact, and show genuine interest. Reflect back what you're hearing to ensure understanding: "So, it sounds like you're feeling frustrated because you couldn't finish your project?" This simple act validates their feelings and fosters a sense of being heard, a cornerstone of healthy communication. Don't interrupt; allow them to express themselves fully, even if their perspective differs from your own.

With younger children, this might involve getting down to their level, making eye contact, and using simple, clear language. Avoid overwhelming them with lengthy explanations or complex sentences. Instead, focus on using visuals, gestures, and engaging storytelling to convey your message. For instance, if you need your toddler to clean up their toys, instead of simply saying "Clean your toys," you could say, "Let's make a game of it! See who can put away the most toys in one minute!" This playful approach makes the task more appealing and fosters cooperation.

As children enter their pre-teen and teenage years, the communication landscape shifts dramatically. Their cognitive abilities have advanced, and they're grappling with complex emotions and navigating a world far more nuanced than the one they experienced in early childhood. Active listening remains crucial, but it must be coupled with empathy and a willingness to understand their perspective, even if you don't agree with it. This is where patience

truly becomes a virtue. Teenagers often express themselves
indirectly or through subtle cues, requiring you to develop keen observation skills.

Avoid lecturing or giving unsolicited advice. Instead, ask open-ended questions that encourage them to explore their thoughts and feelings. For example, instead of saying "You should have studied harder for the test," try "How did you feel about the test? What was the most challenging part?" This approach encourages self-reflection and allows them to identify their own solutions, fostering a sense of autonomy and responsibility. Remember, they're not seeking solutions as much as they're seeking to be understood. Your role is to provide a safe space for them to express themselves without judgment.

Nonverbal communication also plays a significant role, particularly in resolving conflicts. Your body language –your tone of voice, facial expressions, and posture – speaks volumes. A raised voice, even if accompanied by kind words, can undermine your message. Maintaining calm and composure, even in stressful situations, is crucial. If you find yourself becoming angry or frustrated, take a deep breath, step back, and give yourself time to compose yourself before resuming the conversation.

Effective communication involves teaching your child valuable communication skills as well. This means modeling respectful dialogue, active listening, and assertive communication. Encourage them to express their needs and feelings clearly and respectfully, while teaching them to listen to others without interrupting or dismissing their viewpoints. Role-playing can be a helpful tool in this
process, allowing them to practice expressing themselves in a safe environment.

Furthermore, consider the context of your communication. Avoid having important conversations when you or your child are stressed, tired, or emotionally charged. Choose a time and place that's conducive to calm and open communication. Sometimes, a simple walk together can create a more relaxed atmosphere than a formal sit-down conversation.

Be mindful of your own communication style. Are you a direct communicator or more indirect? Understanding your communication style can help you adapt to your child's needs. If you're a direct communicator, make an effort to soften your approach with your child, especially as they enter their teenage years, and if you tend to communicate indirectly, aim to express yourself more clearly.

Remember that consistency is key. Establish clear expectations for communication within your family. This might involve creating designated times for family discussions or establishing a system for resolving conflicts.

Encourage open communication by making yourselves accessible and available to your children.

Sometimes, despite your best efforts, miscommunication will occur. This is perfectly normal, and it's an opportunity for both you and your child to learn and grow. When a misunderstanding arises, apologize if necessary, and work together to find a resolution. Explain your perspective clearly and respectfully, and encourage your child to do the same.

The use of technology introduces another layer of complexity to communication. While technology can facilitate communication, excessive screen time can detract from face-to-face interaction and hinder the development of essential social skills. Establish clear boundaries regarding screen time, and encourage your children to engage in activities that foster meaningful connections with family and friends. Be aware of the types of digital communication your child is engaged in, and monitor their online interactions to ensure their safety and well-being. The digital world is a realm that demands careful navigation and monitoring from parents.

Moreover, ensure that your communication aligns with your parenting style and values. Inconsistency between your words and actions can cause confusion and undermine your authority. Your communication should reflect your commitment to unconditional love and your dedication to nurturing a healthy parent-child relationship. It's about creating a consistent environment where your child feels safe, understood, and empowered to express themselves. This fosters a sense of trust and security that will serve as their bedrock for many years to come.

Finally, remember that effective communication is an ongoing process, not a destination. As your child grows and changes, so too must your communication strategies. Be flexible, adaptable, and willing to learn and grow along with your child. Embrace the challenges, and celebrate the triumphs. The journey toward effective communication is a testament to the depth and resilience of your parent-child bond. This investment in open and honest communication will yield immense rewards, shaping your child's emotional intelligence, building their confidence, and fostering a stronger, more enduring relationship between you. The rewards are immeasurable; a strong bond built on understanding and mutual respect is a gift that will continue to give throughout their lives.

Building Trust and Security

Building trust and security isn't about grand gestures; it's woven into the fabric of everyday interactions. It's in the quiet moments, the shared laughter, the whispered secrets, and the consistent, unwavering presence of a parent who is truly there. This isn't a passive state; it's an active process requiring consistent effort and self-reflection. Think of it like tending a garden; it demands daily attention, nurturing, and the occasional weeding out of negativity.

One of the most powerful tools in building trust is consistency. Children thrive on predictability. Knowing what to expect – bedtime routines, mealtimes, family activities –provides a sense of stability and security, especially in a world that often feels chaotic and unpredictable. This isn't about rigid adherence to a schedule; flexibility is key. But establishing a general framework within which your child can operate offers a sense of control and reduces anxiety. This sense of control, even in small things, empowers them. Let them choose between two outfits for the day, or involve them in age-appropriate household chores. These small choices build their confidence and sense of agency, contributing significantly to their overall feeling of security.

Furthermore, following through on your promises, big or small, is paramount. If you say you'll read a story before bedtime, do it. If you promise a trip to the park, make it happen. Breaking promises, even seemingly insignificant ones, erodes trust. Children learn to interpret actions more than words, and inconsistent behavior sends a confusing and unsettling message. It tells them that their parent's words are unreliable, creating a subtle but significant crack in the foundation of trust. Building a reputation for dependability takes time, but the rewards are invaluable.

Transparency and honesty are equally vital components of building trust. Children are incredibly perceptive and can often sense when something is amiss, even if you try to hide it. While you don't need to burden them with adult worries, age-appropriate explanations regarding family matters or changes in the household routine foster openness and honesty. This demonstrates respect for their intelligence and capacity to understand, even if the subject matter is difficult. Explaining decisions, even if they don't entirely agree with them, builds a sense of inclusion and understanding. This fosters open communication, making them more likely to approach you with concerns or problems in the future.

Active listening is another essential skill. It's not enough to simply hear your child's words; you need to truly listento their message, paying attention to both verbal and nonverbal cues. This means putting aside distractions, making eye contact, and showing genuine interest in what they have to say. Reflect their feelings back to them: "It sounds like you're really frustrated because..." or "It seems like you're feeling sad because..." This validation of their emotions builds a sense of safety and understanding. It shows that you value their feelings and perspectives, fostering a strong emotional connection. Remember, sometimes children just need to be heard, not necessarily given solutions.

Creating a safe space for emotional expression is crucial. Children need to know that it's okay to express a wide range of emotions – happiness, sadness, anger, fear – without fear of judgment or punishment. Encourage them to articulate their feelings, offering support and understanding rather than dismissing or minimizing their experiences. This doesn't mean condoning inappropriate behavior, but rather validating their feelings while setting clear boundaries regarding how those feelings are expressed. Creating this safe haven for emotional expression enables open communication and allows them to develop healthy coping mechanisms for emotional challenges. It lays the foundation for their emotional intelligence and self-regulation.

Physical affection plays a significant role, particularly in younger children. Hugs, cuddles, and kisses communicate love and security. These physical displays of affection create a sense of comfort and belonging, strengthening the parent-child bond. As children grow older, the nature of physical affection may change, but the importance of physical connection remains. A hand on the shoulder, a comforting pat on the back – these gestures of support communicate care and understanding. It's important to respect their evolving boundaries, however. As they mature, they may become less receptive to public displays of affection and it's crucial to respect these limits.

Spending quality time together is essential. This doesn't necessarily mean expensive outings or elaborate activities.

It's about creating shared experiences, connecting on a personal level, and fostering a sense of belonging. Reading together, playing games, having dinner as a family – these seemingly mundane activities build lasting memories and strengthen the bond. These shared experiences, irrespective of their size, offer opportunities for connection, laughter, and the creation of lasting memories. It's the quality of the time spent, not the quantity, that truly matters. Putting aside screens and other distractions, providing undivided attention, creates space for genuine interaction.

Protecting children from harm, both physical and emotional, is a fundamental parental responsibility. This includes setting clear boundaries, teaching them about safety, and protecting them from exposure to violence, abuse, or neglect. It also involves creating a nurturing environment where they feel safe to express themselves without fear of ridicule or judgment. This protection extends to the online world,
actively monitoring their online activities and educating them about the potential dangers of the internet. In essence, establishing a secure environment that protects them from physical and emotional threats is an act of profound love and trust.

However, trust isn't a one-way street. It's a reciprocal relationship that requires effort from both parents and children. Parents need to model trustworthiness in their own actions and interactions, demonstrating honesty, integrity, and reliability in their dealings with their children and others. Children, in turn, need to learn to be responsible, to communicate honestly, and to respect the boundaries that are set. This reciprocal relationship requires constant nurturing and understanding from both sides.

Remember, the parent-child relationship is a living, evolving entity. It changes and adapts as children grow and mature. What works for a toddler may not work for a teenager. The key is to remain flexible, adaptable, and willing to adjust your approach as needed. Being present, listening actively, and showing unconditional love are the cornerstones upon which trust and security are built. It's a continuous process of learning, adapting, and growing together. The journey may have its challenges, but the destination—a strong, loving, and trusting parent-child bond—is more than worth the effort. It's a legacy of love that will last a lifetime, shaping the individual's character and their ability to build healthy relationships throughout their lives. It's about building a solid foundation, brick by brick, ensuring that the bond between parent and child remains unshaken, even when faced with life's inevitable storms. This foundation, built on trust and security, provides a safe harbor, a place of refuge where the child can always return, knowing they are loved, accepted, and understood.

Creating a Safe and Supportive Environment

Building a safe and supportive environment isn't about achieving a picture-perfect family; it's about cultivating a space where imperfections are embraced, mistakes are learning opportunities, and love is the unwavering constant. It's about fostering a sense of belonging, where each member feels valued, respected, and unconditionally loved, regardless of their flaws or achievements. This involves creating a haven, a sanctuary from the harsh realities of the outside world, where children can freely express themselves without fear of judgment or reprisal.

This sanctuary begins with establishing clear and consistent boundaries. These aren't rigid walls designed to stifle individuality; rather, they are the sturdy framework upon which a child's sense of security is built. Boundaries provide a sense of order and predictability, reducing anxiety and promoting emotional stability. Think of them as the guardrails on a rollercoaster – they're there to ensure safety and prevent disaster, but they also allow for thrilling experiences within a controlled environment. These
boundaries should be age-appropriate and consistently enforced, ensuring fairness and understanding. A child who understands the rules feels safer, even when those rules limit their immediate desires. Inconsistency, on the other hand, breeds confusion and undermines the parent-child bond. A child who never knows what to expect feels insecure and anxious, leading to potential behavioral problems.

Beyond consistent boundaries, open communication is paramount. It's not enough to simply tell children the rules; they need to understand the reasoning behind them. This requires active listening, where parents truly hear, not just listen to, their children's concerns and perspectives. Creating a space where children feel comfortable sharing their thoughts and feelings, even the difficult ones, is crucial.

Encourage open dialogue, even about sensitive subjects, fostering a relationship based on mutual respect and understanding. Ask open-ended questions, listen attentively without interrupting, and validate their feelings, even if you don't agree with their actions. Remember, the goal isn't to win every argument; it's to build a strong, trusting relationship. Sometimes, simply acknowledging their feelings and offering comfort is enough. A simple, "I understand you're feeling frustrated," can make a world of difference.

Family meetings can be invaluable tools for fostering communication and collaboration. These aren't formal sessions; they're relaxed gatherings where family members can discuss issues, share ideas, and make decisions together.

They provide a platform for children to express their opinions, fostering a sense of agency and empowerment. Rotating the responsibility of leading the meeting amongst family members teaches valuable skills in leadership, communication, and problem-solving. This shared decision-making process promotes a sense of collective responsibility, making children feel more invested in their family's well-being. These discussions shouldn't solely focus on problem-solving; they should also include fun activities, shared stories, and moments of connection. The aim is to strengthen the family unit, not just address conflicts.

Prioritizing quality time is another crucial element in building a supportive environment. In today's busy world, it's easy to get caught up in the whirlwind of schedules and responsibilities, neglecting the precious moments of connection with our children. However, these seemingly insignificant moments hold immense power in nurturing the parent-child bond. It's not necessarily about extravagant outings or expensive gifts; it's about shared experiences, be it reading together before bedtime, playing a board game, or simply engaging in a meaningful conversation. These shared activities create lasting memories and strengthen the emotional bond between parents and children. Consider establishing regular family rituals, like weekly game nights or Sunday brunches, to create a sense of routine and consistency. These traditions create a sense of belonging and reinforce the importance of family unity.

Incorporating acts of kindness and service into family life fosters empathy and compassion. Volunteering together at a local charity, helping a neighbor in need, or simply performing small acts of kindness within the family can create a profound impact on children's development. These experiences teach children the importance of giving back and contributing to the wider community. It also reinforces the notion of interdependence and mutual support, strengthening their understanding of their role within the family unit. Children who learn to give and serve often develop stronger empathy skills, fostering their ability to connect with others on a deeper level.

Finally, creating a safe and supportive environment is not just about the things we do; it's also about the things we refrain from. Excessive criticism, harsh punishments, and constant comparisons can erode a child's self-esteem and damage the parent-child relationship. Instead, focus on positive reinforcement, celebrating their successes, and providing constructive feedback when necessary. Remember that children are works in progress; they are constantly learning and growing. Embrace their imperfections and celebrate their uniqueness. Encourage them to take risks, to make mistakes, and to learn from their experiences. A supportive parent is not a perfect parent; they are a parent who is willing to learn, adapt, and grow alongside their child. They are a parent who provides unconditional love and support, even amidst challenges and disagreements. This unwavering support forms the bedrock of a strong parent-child bond, a legacy of love that will endure throughout their lives.

Creating this nurturing environment requires conscious effort, self-reflection, and a willingness to adapt. It's a journey, not a destination, and requires ongoing adjustments as children grow and their needs evolve. There will be setbacks, moments of frustration, and times when we feel we've fallen short. But it's these very moments that remind us of the importance of perseverance and the power of

unconditional love. The rewards – a strong, loving, and supportive family – are immeasurable, shaping not only the lives of our children but also our own. The foundation of trust and security built through these efforts will serve as a beacon of hope and stability, guiding them through life's inevitable storms and enabling them to build strong and healthy relationships in their own lives. It's an investment in their future, and ultimately, an investment in our own happiness and fulfillment as parents. Remember that the journey of parenting is a continuous learning process; embrace the challenges, celebrate the victories, and always prioritize the bond you share with your child. The strength of that bond will withstand the test of time and leave an

indelible mark on the hearts and lives of everyone involved.

FIVE

SCREEN TIME MANAGEMENT

The digital world is a double-edged sword. It offers incredible opportunities for learning, connection, and entertainment, yet it also presents significant challenges to parents striving to raise well-adjusted children. The constant pull of screens, the addictive nature of certain apps, and the sheer volume of information available can overwhelm both parents and children, leading to conflict and unhealthy habits. Managing screen time effectively isn't about eliminating technology altogether; it's about creating a balanced approach that prioritizes real-life experiences, healthy relationships, and overall well-being.

The first step in effective screen time management is understanding your child's age and developmental stage. A five-year-old's engagement with technology will differ drastically from a fifteen-year-old's. What's appropriate for a young child learning basic literacy skills through interactive apps might be detrimental to a teenager already struggling with social media pressures and cyberbullying. Consider the content they're consuming. Is it educational, entertaining, or simply mindlessly stimulating? Passive consumption of videos, for example, offers little in the way of cognitive stimulation or social interaction compared to engaging in interactive games or online learning platforms.

Establishing clear guidelines is crucial. These aren't about rigid rules, but rather about creating a family media plan. This plan should be age-appropriate, collaborative (involving your child as much as possible, depending on their age), and consistently enforced. Start by defining specific time limits for screen use. This might involve setting a daily limit, a weekly limit, or even a schedule dictating specific times of the day when screen time is permitted. Make it clear what types of activities are acceptable during screen time and which are not. For younger children, this might mean focusing on educational apps or age-appropriate shows, while older children might have more autonomy, but within clearly defined boundaries.

Consider the location of screens. Banning screens from bedrooms is a common and effective strategy, as it prevents late-night screen use which disrupts sleep patterns.

Establishing screen-free zones, such as the dining table or family gathering areas, encourages face-to-face communication and strengthens family bonds. These zones create opportunities for genuine interaction and prevent the distraction of screens from important family moments.

Dinner time, for instance, should be a screen-free zone to allow for conversation and connection. These moments are crucial for fostering emotional intelligence and strengthening family relationships.

Active parental involvement is key. Don't just passively allow your child to use screens; engage with them in their digital activities. Play games with them, watch educational videos together, or help them navigate online learning platforms. This approach not only fosters a closer parent-child bond but also allows you to monitor their online activities, ensuring they're using technology responsibly and safely. This active participation also allows you to model healthy digital habits and emphasize the importance of
balance.

Open communication is essential. Talk to your children about their online experiences. Ask them what they're watching, playing, or interacting with online. Encourage them to share their feelings about their online interactions, both positive and negative. This open dialogue creates a safe space for them to discuss any issues they may be facing, such as cyberbullying, online predators, or pressure to conform to unrealistic online standards. By fostering this open communication, you can identify potential problems early and intervene effectively.

Model healthy technology use yourself. Children learn by observing the adults in their lives. If they see you constantly glued to your phone or spending hours scrolling through social media, they're likely to emulate this behavior. By modeling healthy habits, you set a positive example and teach them the importance of balance in their own lives. This means setting your own boundaries on screen time and prioritizing face-to-face interactions and offline activities.

Technology can be a tool for learning and connection, but it shouldn't dominate your child's life. Encourage participation in offline activities – sports, hobbies, creative pursuits, and social interactions with friends and family. These activities foster development in critical thinking, problem-solving, creativity and emotional intelligence. A healthy balance between online and offline activities contributes to a well-rounded life.

Remember, screen time limits are not a punishment; they are a tool to help your children develop healthy habits and maintain a balanced lifestyle. It's important to create a positive and supportive environment, teaching children the importance of digital wellness rather than imposing strict rules that breed resentment and rebellion. Consider offering rewards for responsible screen time use and implementing a system of consequences for exceeding limits. Positive reinforcement encourages compliance and fosters a sense of responsibility.

The transition from excessive screen time to a balanced approach requires patience and consistency. There will be challenges and setbacks along the way, but persistence is key. Don't expect immediate changes; it's a gradual process requiring consistent effort and communication. Remember, this isn't just about limiting screen time; it's about nurturing healthy habits, fostering strong relationships, and creating a supportive environment where your children can thrive.

Technology is constantly evolving, so your strategies for managing screen time need to adapt accordingly. Stay informed about new apps, trends, and potential risks. Participate in workshops, read articles, or speak to other parents about effective strategies. Regularly review and adjust your family media plan to keep it relevant and effective.

Think about creating a "Digital Detox" day each week, or even just a couple of hours each day, where screens are completely off-limits. Encourage family game nights, outdoor activities, reading, or engaging in creative pursuits.

This time away from screens allows for family bonding, relaxation and improved mental health for both parents and children. Use this time to reconnect, engage in meaningful conversations, and foster a stronger parent-child bond.

Finally, remember to be empathetic and understanding. The digital world is a significant part of your child's life, and navigating it successfully requires collaboration, open communication, and a willingness to adapt. Your role is to guide them, not to control them. By working together, you can help your children develop healthy relationships with technology, fostering a balanced and fulfilling life both online and off. This journey requires patience, consistency, and a deep understanding of your child's individual needs and developmental stage. Remember, your goal is to foster responsible technology use, not to eliminate it entirely. A balanced approach is the key to successfully navigating the digital world and raising well-adjusted, happy children.

Digital Literacy and Safety

The previous chapter emphasized the importance of balance in our children's lives, particularly concerning screen time. But simply limiting access isn't enough. We must also equip our children with the knowledge and skills to navigate the digital world safely and responsibly. This isn't about shielding them from technology – a nearly impossible task in today's world – but rather about empowering them to become discerning and informed digital citizens. Think of it as teaching them to swim, not keeping them out of the water entirely.

The digital world is a vast and often confusing landscape. It's a place where information flows freely, sometimes accurately, sometimes not. It's a place of connection, but also of potential isolation. It's a place of immense creativity and entertainment, but also of potential danger. Our children need to learn to discern between these aspects, to appreciate the positive while mitigating the negative. This requires a multi-faceted approach, beginning with open and honest conversations.

Start by talking to your children about the internet and social media at an age-appropriate level. Begin these conversations early, even before they have significant online access. Don't wait until a problem arises; proactive education is far more effective. Explain the concept of online privacy – that not everything they see or share should be shared publicly.

Discuss the difference between sharing with friends and sharing with strangers, emphasizing the importance of discretion and caution. Use relatable analogies; compare online interactions to real-world interactions, emphasizing that the same rules of politeness, respect, and safety apply in both contexts.

As your children get older, the conversations need to become more nuanced. Discuss the potential dangers of cyberbullying, online predators, and inappropriate content.

Explain how to identify and report such incidents, emphasizing that they should always tell a trusted adult if they encounter something upsetting or concerning online.

Encourage them to be critical thinkers, to question the information they encounter online and to verify its authenticity through multiple sources. Teach them to identify misleading information, propaganda, and fake news, crucial skills in an era of rampant misinformation.

Beyond conversations, practical measures are vital. Set up parental controls on devices and use monitoring software responsibly. These tools aren't about spying but about providing a safety net and allowing you to guide your children's online experiences. It's about building trust and establishing clear boundaries, not about creating an atmosphere of suspicion. Remember to explain the rationale behind these controls, making them feel involved in the process rather than subjected to arbitrary rules. Regularly review these settings and adapt them as your children mature and their digital literacy improves.

Digital literacy extends beyond simply avoiding danger; it also encompasses responsible online behavior. Teach your children about online etiquette – the importance of being polite and respectful in online interactions, just as they would be in face-to-face conversations. Discuss the consequences of their actions online – that their digital footprint can last a lifetime and impact future opportunities.

Emphasize the importance of thinking before posting, commenting, or sharing anything online. A moment of impulsivity can have lasting consequences, both personally and professionally.

Furthermore, instill a sense of digital citizenship in your children. Encourage them to be responsible users of technology, to be mindful of their online actions, and to contribute positively to the online community. Discuss the importance of respecting intellectual property, of not plagiarizing, and of giving credit where credit is due. Encourage them to participate in online communities in a positive and constructive manner, avoiding negativity and contributing thoughtfully to discussions.

Beyond the practical, focus on cultivating critical thinking skills. Help your children learn to evaluate information sources, identify bias, and recognize misinformation. Teach them to cross-reference information from multiple sources, to consider different perspectives, and to develop their own informed opinions. In today's digital world, the ability to critically evaluate information is as important as the ability to access it. This is a skill that will serve them well throughout their lives, not just online.

Another crucial aspect of digital literacy is privacy. Teach children the importance of protecting their personal information online. Explain why they shouldn't share sensitive information such as their address, phone number, or passwords with strangers. Emphasize the importance of creating strong passwords and keeping them secure. Discuss the risks associated with sharing personal information on social media or other online platforms. Teach them to be cautious about accepting friend requests from strangers and to report any suspicious activity.

Finally, model responsible digital citizenship yourself. Children learn by observing their parents. If you spend hours scrolling through social media, constantly checking your phone, or engaging in unproductive online activities, your children are likely to follow suit. Show them that technology is a tool, not a master. Prioritize real-life interactions and experiences. Engage in activities together that don't involve screens. Create a family culture that values balance, connection, and mindful technology use.

This journey of guiding our children through the digital world is a continuous process, requiring ongoing communication, adaptation, and a willingness to learn alongside them. It's a journey of education and empowerment, equipping them not just to survive, but to thrive in the complex digital landscape. Remember, the goal isn't to eliminate technology from their lives but to help them harness its power responsibly, ethically, and safely. By fostering a culture of open communication, responsible use, and critical thinking, we can help our children navigate the digital world with confidence and maturity, creating a strong foundation for a fulfilling and successful future. The digital world is not a threat; it's a reality, and equipping our children to navigate it effectively is our responsibility as parents. It is a journey that demands our continued involvement and commitment, but one that promises significant rewards in the long run. By teaching them the skills to navigate this complex world, we are not only protecting them from harm, but we're empowering them to become responsible and informed digital citizens. This is an investment in their future, a gift that will continue to give long after they leave our homes. It requires patience, understanding, and a commitment to ongoing learning. But the rewards – a child equipped to thrive in the digital age – are immeasurable. By approaching digital literacy with this comprehensive and proactive strategy, parents can equip their children with the skills and knowledge necessary to navigate the digital world safely and responsibly, setting them up for a successful and fulfilling future. This ongoing dialogue and adaptation are vital to ensuring that our children not only survive but flourish in the ever-evolving digital landscape. The key is not to fear technology but to embrace it thoughtfully, guiding our children to utilize its potential while mitigating its inherent risks.

Promoting Healthy Online Habits

The digital world offers incredible opportunities for learning, connection, and creativity. However, its very accessibility also presents significant challenges, particularly for developing minds. Simply limiting screen time, as discussed in the previous chapter, is only one piece of a much larger puzzle. True digital well-being requires a proactive and comprehensive approach, focusing on fostering healthy online habits and equipping our children with the critical thinking skills necessary to navigate the complexities of the internet safely and responsibly.

This involves more than just setting time limits; it's about cultivating a culture of open communication, where children feel comfortable discussing their online experiences, both positive and negative, without fear of judgment or punishment. Creating this safe space for dialogue is crucial.

Think of it as building a bridge of trust, allowing them to approach you with questions, concerns, or even just to share something exciting they encountered online. This open dialogue paves the way for effective guidance and support.

One vital aspect is teaching media literacy. Children need to understand that not everything they see online is true or accurate. This involves teaching them how to evaluate sources, identify bias, and recognize misinformation. We can achieve this through engaging discussions, role-playing scenarios, and utilizing age-appropriate resources that illustrate the difference between reliable and unreliable information sources. A simple example would be analyzing different news articles on the same topic, comparing their perspectives and identifying potential biases. Encourage them to ask questions: Who created this information? What is their motive? Is there evidence to support their claims? These critical questions are the building blocks of media literacy.

Furthermore, we need to help our children understand the concept of digital footprints. Every online interaction, every post, every comment, leaves a digital trail. This isn't just about privacy; it's about responsibility. They need to understand the long-term implications of their online actions and the potential consequences of sharing inappropriate content or engaging in cyberbullying. Openly discussing the permanence of online information and the potential ramifications for their future can instill a sense of responsibility and caution. Real-life examples of individuals facing consequences for their online actions can be powerful teaching tools. We can use these examples to help them understand the weight of their digital actions and the importance of making responsible choices.

Cyberbullying is a significant concern in today's digital landscape. It's crucial to educate our children about the different forms of cyberbullying, such as online harassment, threats, and exclusion. Equally important is teaching them how to respond appropriately if they become victims or witnesses to cyberbullying. This includes encouraging them to report incidents to trusted adults, such as parents, teachers, or school counselors. Role-playing scenarios can help children practice how to respond to cyberbullying calmly and assertively, emphasizing the importance of seeking help rather than retaliating. Emphasize the importance of reporting, not only for their safety but also for the well-being of others who may be facing similar situations.

Another critical area is online safety. Children need to understand the risks associated with sharing personal information online, such as their address, phone number, or school. We can teach them about the importance of strong passwords, the dangers of clicking on suspicious links, and the need to be cautious about communicating with strangers online. This includes explaining the difference between private and public information and encouraging them to think before they share. Using age-appropriate resources, games, or interactive activities can make these lessons engaging and memorable. Regular check-ins and open discussions can solidify these lessons and create an environment where they feel comfortable sharing any concerns.

Beyond safety, it's equally important to cultivate a balanced approach to technology. We should encourage children to participate in a wide range of activities, both online and offline. This involves nurturing interests in sports, arts, music, reading, and other offline pursuits. A balanced lifestyle ensures that technology complements, rather than dominates, their lives. This approach helps prevent excessive screen time and fosters a well-rounded development.

Encouraging family time, engaging in outdoor activities, and participating in community events are all excellent strategies to cultivate this balance.

Furthermore, modeling healthy online habits is paramount. Children learn by observing the behavior of their parents and caregivers. If we spend excessive time scrolling through social media or constantly checking our phones, our children are more likely to adopt these habits. By demonstrating responsible technology use, we are setting a positive example for our children to follow. This includes setting boundaries for ourselves, being mindful of our screen time, and engaging in offline activities that promote healthy family interactions.

Finally, remember that this is an ongoing process, not a one-time lecture. Regularly revisiting these topics, adapting our approach as our children grow and mature, and engaging in ongoing conversations are vital. The digital landscape is constantly evolving, and our approach to educating our children must evolve with it. It is a journey of continuous learning and adaptation, requiring our active participation and commitment. The goal is not to eliminate technology from their lives, but to equip them with the skills and knowledge to navigate it responsibly, ethically, and safely –empowering them to thrive in the ever-evolving digital world. This consistent effort will not only safeguard them but also nurture their growth into responsible and informed digital citizens. The investment in their digital literacy today is an investment in their future success and well-being. The journey may be challenging, but the rewards are

immeasurable. By fostering healthy online habits and open communication, we can guide our children towards a brighter, safer, and more fulfilling digital future.

SIX

BALANCING TECHNOLOGY AND REAL-LIFE INTERACTIONS

The previous chapter focused on setting boundaries around screen time, but limiting access isn't the whole solution. True digital well-being necessitates a more nuanced approach, one that integrates technology thoughtfully into a life rich with real-world experiences and genuine human connection.

Think of it not as a battle against screens, but a careful choreography where technology plays a supporting, not leading, role. The challenge lies in finding that delicate equilibrium, ensuring that the digital world complements, rather than supplants, the vibrant tapestry of real-life interactions.

One of the most effective strategies is to consciously cultivate "unplugged" time. This doesn't simply mean turning off devices; it means creating dedicated spaces and periods where screens are entirely absent. Designate specific times each day – perhaps an hour before bedtime, or a couple of hours on weekends – as technology-free zones. These periods should be filled with activities that encourage face-to-face interaction and engagement with the physical world. Family dinners, board game nights, outdoor adventures, reading together – these are the building blocks of strong family bonds and a balanced life. The key is to make these unplugged periods appealing and engaging, so children actively choose to participate. Consider creating a family "unplugged box," filled with ideas for activities to do together without screens.

The transition from screen time to real-life engagement shouldn't be abrupt; it should be gradual and carefully managed. Rather than suddenly imposing strict limits, gently guide your child towards more balanced habits. Start by reducing screen time incrementally, replacing some screen activities with alternatives that encourage interaction and exploration. This could involve replacing an evening of video games with a family bike ride, a visit to the park, or a creative project together. Involve your child in the planning process; let them suggest activities that they find engaging and fun. This collaborative approach makes the transition smoother and less likely to result in resistance.

Beyond scheduled unplugged time, it's crucial to be mindful of how technology permeates the rest of the day. Constant connectivity can subtly erode the quality of real-life interactions. Imagine a family dinner punctuated by the incessant pinging of phones, or a conversation interrupted by a child's preoccupation with a tablet. These fragmented interactions fail to foster the deep connections that are essential for emotional development. Establish clear expectations around phone usage during family time, emphasizing the importance of being present and engaged. Teach your children to be mindful of their own behavior and the impact it has on others. Encourage them to prioritize real-life interactions over digital distractions.

The creation of shared experiences is paramount. These shared experiences solidify family bonds and create lasting memories. Regularly engage in activities that bring the family together, fostering a sense of belonging and connection. Weekend trips, family game nights, volunteering together – these shared experiences offer opportunities for laughter, conversation, and the creation of cherished memories. They also serve as powerful counterpoints to the solitary nature of many digital activities. The focus should be on creating opportunities for meaningful interaction, not just filling the time with activities.

Furthermore, we need to be mindful of the subtle ways technology can undermine real-life skills. Children who spend excessive time in virtual worlds may develop difficulties in social situations, lacking the practice in navigating complex social dynamics. They may struggle with emotional regulation, empathy, and nonverbal communication. To counteract this, actively encourage participation in activities that promote social interaction and skill development. Enroll your child in team sports, music lessons, or community groups – activities that provide opportunities to collaborate, communicate, and build

relationships. These real-world experiences provide invaluable opportunities for learning and growth, developing skills that extend far beyond the digital realm.

Another significant consideration is the impact of technology on attention span and focus. The constant stream of information and stimulation from screens can lead to shorter attention spans and difficulty with sustained concentration.

To mitigate this, encourage activities that require focused attention and sustained effort. Reading books, working on puzzles, engaging in creative hobbies – these activities help train the brain to focus and concentrate for longer periods, skills crucial for academic success and overall well-being.

Introduce these activities gradually, starting with shorter periods and gradually increasing the duration. It's also essential to model healthy digital habits. Children learn by observing, and if they see their parents constantly glued to their screens, they're more likely to emulate that behavior. Practice what you preach. Put your phone away during meals and family time, and actively engage in conversations without distractions. Show them the value of disconnecting and being present in the moment. Your own behavior serves as a powerful example, shaping their understanding of healthy technology usage.

Moreover, teaching children digital literacy and responsible online behavior is crucial. This goes beyond simply setting boundaries and limiting screen time. It involves equipping them with the knowledge and skills to navigate the online world safely and responsibly. Teach them about online safety, privacy, cyberbullying, and responsible social media usage. Discuss the importance of critical thinking and media literacy, encouraging them to question the information they encounter online. Equip them with the tools to identify misinformation and navigate the complexities of the digital landscape responsibly.

Finally, remember that the balance between technology and real-life interactions is an ongoing process, not a destination. Regularly revisit these strategies, adjusting your approach as your children grow and their needs evolve. Engage in open and honest conversations about technology use, listening to your child's concerns and perspectives. Create a supportive and collaborative environment where technology is viewed as a tool to enhance life, not replace it. The aim isn't to eliminate technology entirely, but to ensure it serves a supportive, enriching role within a life rich with meaningful relationships and real-world experiences. This ongoing dialogue and adaptation are key to fostering a healthy and balanced relationship with technology throughout your child's development. The effort you invest today will yield immeasurable rewards in the years to come.

The Importance of Offline Activities

The digital world, with its alluring glow and endless possibilities, can easily overshadow the simple joys of offline life. We've discussed the crucial need for balanced screen time, but simply restricting access isn't enough. To truly nurture a child's holistic development, we must actively cultivate a rich tapestry of offline experiences. These aren't merely alternatives to screen time; they are the very foundation upon which a well-rounded, emotionally resilient individual is built.

Think back to your own childhood. What are your most cherished memories? Chances are, many involve the tangible, the sensory, the deeply human connections forged outside the digital realm. The thrill of building a magnificent sandcastle only to watch the tide wash it away, the exhilaration of climbing a tree and feeling the wind in your hair, the warmth of laughter shared around a campfire, the quiet contentment of reading a book nestled in a sunbeam –these are the experiences that shape us, that foster creativity, empathy, and resilience.

These offline activities aren't just fun; they are crucial for a child's development on multiple levels. Outdoor play, for instance, fosters physical fitness and coordination. It's not just about burning energy; it's about developing gross motor skills, spatial awareness, and problem-solving abilities. Climbing a jungle gym requires strategic thinking, assessing risks, and planning movements. Building a fort in the woods cultivates creativity, resourcefulness, and collaboration. The unstructured nature of outdoor play allows children to explore their own imaginations, develop their own rules, and negotiate conflicts – all vital social and emotional skills.

Beyond the physical benefits, outdoor play has profound implications for mental well-being. Exposure to sunlight boosts Vitamin D levels, crucial for bone health and mood regulation. Nature itself offers a calming influence, reducing stress and anxiety. Studies have shown that children who spend more time in nature exhibit lower levels of ADHD symptoms and improved attention spans. Ironically, the very thing many parents turn to screens for – calming their children – can often be achieved more effectively through the restorative power of the natural world.

Family time, another crucial offline activity, is the glue that binds families together. This doesn't mean rigidly scheduled events; it's about creating shared experiences and memories.

A family game night, a weekend hike, a meal cooked and shared together – these seemingly simple activities foster a sense of belonging, build strong family bonds, and provide opportunities for meaningful communication. During these moments, children learn about family history, traditions, and values. They observe how adults interact, learn conflict resolution skills, and develop a sense of security and stability.

Consider the value of creative pursuits. Drawing, painting, sculpting, playing a musical instrument – these activities nurture imagination, self-expression, and fine motor skills.

They provide an outlet for emotions, a means of communication that transcends words. The act of creating something tangible, something beautiful, instills a sense of accomplishment and self-esteem. These creative outlets can also be deeply therapeutic, providing a healthy way to process emotions and experiences.

Reading, too, deserves a prominent place in a child's offline world. The benefits of reading extend far beyond literacy skills. It fosters imagination, empathy, critical thinking, and vocabulary development. Reading exposes children to different cultures, perspectives, and ideas, broadening their horizons and nurturing their intellectual curiosity. Reading aloud to children, especially before bedtime, creates a warm and nurturing atmosphere, fostering a strong parent-child bond. It's a time for shared intimacy and connection, a ritual that can last a lifetime.

Community involvement offers another avenue for enriching offline experiences. Volunteering at a local animal shelter, participating in a community garden, or joining a sports team– these activities teach children about social responsibility, empathy, and teamwork. They provide opportunities to interact with people from different backgrounds, learn about different perspectives, and develop a sense of civic engagement. These experiences foster a sense of belonging and purpose, contributing to a child's overall well-being. But how do we navigate this delicate balance in a world saturated with technology? It's not about a complete digital detox, but about intentional choices. We need to create a culture within our families that values offline experiences just as much, if not more than, screen time. This requires conscious effort and planning. Schedule regular family game nights, dedicate time for outdoor adventures, and make reading aloud a daily ritual. Turn off the screens during meal times and create designated "screen-free" zones within the home. The key is to make offline activities engaging and appealing.

Don't simply dictate what your child should do; involve them in the planning process. Let them choose the activities they want to engage in, whether it's building a Lego castle, playing board games, or exploring a nearby park. Make it an adventure, a shared experience, rather than a chore.

Furthermore, it's essential to model the behavior we want to see in our children. If we are constantly glued to our screens, our children will likely follow suit. By demonstrating a balanced approach to technology and actively engaging in offline activities ourselves, we create a culture within our families that values real-world experiences.

Remember, the goal is not to eliminate technology entirely, but to integrate it thoughtfully into a life rich with real-world interactions. The digital world can be a powerful tool for learning and connection, but it should never replace the irreplaceable richness of face-to-face interactions, the tangible experiences, and the deeply human connections that are the foundation of a well-balanced and fulfilling life. By consciously cultivating a life rich in offline activities, we equip our children not just with skills, but with the resilience, empathy, and emotional intelligence they need to thrive in an increasingly complex world. This investment in their offline lives will yield dividends far beyond the digital realm, shaping them into well-rounded, happy, and successful individuals. The time spent unplugged will be the time they remember most fondly, the time that truly shaped their lives and created the strongest memories. Investing in their offline world is investing in their future.

Teaching Coping Mechanisms

Equipping children with effective coping mechanisms isn't about shielding them from life's inevitable bumps and bruises; it's about giving them the tools to navigate those challenges with resilience and grace. Think of it like teaching them to swim – you wouldn't just throw them into the deep end and hope for the best. You'd start with the basics, gradually building their confidence and skillset until they can handle any current. This is precisely the approach we need to take when teaching our children how to cope.

The foundation of any effective coping strategy is emotional literacy. Before children can manage their emotions, they need to understand them. Start by labeling feelings. Instead of simply saying "You're upset," try, "You seem frustrated because the blocks aren't working the way you want." This helps children connect their internal experience with specific words and allows them to articulate their emotions more clearly. Use picture books, age-appropriate videos, or even simple games to explore different emotions, discussing how each one might feel in the body and the situations that might trigger them.

Once children can identify their emotions, teach them simple techniques to manage them. Deep breathing exercises are incredibly powerful, even for young children. Make it fun!

Pretend you're blowing out birthday candles, or imagine you're a superhero filling your lungs with power. Guided imagery can also be a valuable tool. Guide your child to visualize a calm and peaceful place – a beach, a forest, or their favorite cozy spot. Encourage them to describe the sights, sounds, and smells of this place, focusing on the calming sensations.

For older children, introduce more sophisticated coping strategies such as progressive muscle relaxation. This technique involves systematically tensing and releasing different muscle groups, helping to reduce physical tension associated with stress. Start with the toes, gradually moving up the body, teaching your child to notice the difference between tension and relaxation. Journaling can be another helpful tool. It provides a safe space for children to express their thoughts and feelings without judgment. Even young children can draw or dictate their feelings into a journal.

Remember, the key is to make these coping strategies part of your child's everyday life, not just something they pull out during a crisis. Practice these techniques regularly, even when your child isn't stressed. This helps them to build a repertoire of skills and develop a sense of self-efficacy – the belief that they can manage their emotions and handle challenging situations.

Beyond emotional regulation, it's crucial to build children's problem-solving skills. Don't rush to solve their problems for them. Instead, guide them through a structured process: first, help them identify the problem clearly; then, brainstorm possible solutions together; next, evaluate the pros and cons of each solution; finally, help them choose a solution and implement it. This empowers them to take control of their lives and develop a sense of agency.

Another vital component of resilience is fostering a strong sense of self-esteem. Children who believe in themselves are better equipped to handle setbacks. Praise their effort, not just their achievements. Focus on their growth and progress, rather than comparing them to others. Help them identify their strengths and celebrate their unique talents. Encourage

them to try new things, even if they're afraid of failure. Embrace mistakes as opportunities for learning and growth.

Building resilience also involves teaching children the importance of seeking support. Let them know that it's okay to ask for help when they need it. Model this behavior yourself; let them see you seeking support from friends, family, or professionals when you're struggling. Encourage them to talk about their feelings and concerns, creating a safe and open space where they feel comfortable sharing. This could involve family meetings, regular check-ins, or simply making time for relaxed conversations.

Remember, building resilience is a gradual process, not a quick fix. It requires patience, consistency, and a deep understanding of your child's unique needs and personality.

There's no one-size-fits-all solution. What works for one child might not work for another. Be flexible, adapt your approach as needed, and celebrate every small victory along the way.

Consider the example of a child struggling with test anxiety.

Instead of simply telling them to "calm down," guide them through a structured approach. Help them identify the specific aspects of the test that cause anxiety. Is it the pressure to perform well? The fear of failure? The unfamiliar format? Once they've pinpointed the root cause, brainstorm coping mechanisms together. Perhaps they could practice relaxation techniques before the test, break down the study material into manageable chunks, or visualize themselves succeeding. Each small step forward builds confidence and reduces anxiety.

Or think about a child facing social challenges. They may be struggling to make friends or feeling excluded. Instead of offering simplistic advice like "just be yourself," help them explore the specific dynamics of their social interactions. Role-playing different scenarios can be incredibly valuable. Practice initiating conversations, responding to teasing, or resolving conflicts. Encourage them to join clubs or
activities that align with their interests, creating opportunities to connect with like-minded peers.

Building resilience isn't just about equipping children with coping mechanisms; it's about cultivating a mindset of hope and optimism. Teach them to focus on their strengths, celebrate their successes, and view setbacks as opportunities for growth. Encourage them to develop a sense of gratitude, appreciating the positive aspects of their lives, even during difficult times. These skills are essential not just for
navigating childhood challenges but for thriving throughout life.

Incorporate resilience-building into everyday routines. For instance, during family dinner, engage in gratitude exercises, where each member shares something they're thankful for. This fosters positive emotions and strengthens family bonds. When your child faces a minor setback, like losing a game, encourage them to reflect on what they learned and how they can improve next time, instead of focusing solely on the outcome.

Furthermore, understand that resilience isn't a static trait; it's a dynamic process that evolves throughout life. As children grow and encounter new challenges, their coping mechanisms may need to adapt. Remain open to exploring new strategies and learning alongside your child. It's a collaborative journey, emphasizing open communication and mutual support.

Remember that seeking professional help is a sign of strength, not weakness. If your child is struggling to cope with stress or adversity, don't hesitate to seek guidance from a therapist or counselor. They can provide specialized support and teach you more advanced coping mechanisms tailored to your child's specific needs.

Ultimately, teaching coping mechanisms is about empowering children to become self-sufficient, resourceful, and emotionally intelligent individuals. It's about providing them with the tools they need not just to survive life's inevitable challenges, but to thrive in the face of adversity. This is a journey that will last a lifetime, and your consistent effort will shape your child's capacity for resilience,
empowering them to navigate life's currents with confidence and grace. The investment is immeasurable, and the rewards are the gift of a strong, adaptable, and flourishing child.

Fostering Self-Esteem

Building a child's resilience isn't solely about equipping them with coping mechanisms; it's also about fostering a deep-seated belief in their own worth. Self-esteem, that inner compass guiding them through life's uncertainties, is the bedrock upon which resilience is built. Without a strong sense of self, coping mechanisms can feel like flimsy rafts in a stormy sea – potentially effective, but ultimately insufficient. A child who believes in their inherent value is more likely to bounce back from setbacks, to view challenges as opportunities for growth, and to navigate the inevitable disappointments with a sense of inner strength.

This journey toward fostering self-esteem isn't a sprint; it's a marathon requiring consistent effort, unwavering support, and a deep understanding of your child's unique personality and needs. It's not about showering them with empty praise; it's about cultivating genuine self-awareness and a realistic understanding of their strengths and weaknesses. It's about nurturing their individuality, celebrating their achievements, and providing a safe space for them to explore their vulnerabilities without fear of judgment.

One of the most effective ways to build self-esteem is through unconditional love and acceptance. This doesn't mean passively accepting every behavior; it means accepting your child as a unique individual, flaws and all. Let them know, unequivocally, that your love is not contingent on their accomplishments or their adherence to some idealized standard of perfection. This unwavering support provides a secure base from which they can explore the world, take risks, and learn from their mistakes without the crippling fear of losing your love. Regularly express your love and appreciation, not just through grand gestures, but through small, everyday acts of affection – a hug, a shared laugh, a listening ear.

Beyond unconditional love, fostering self-esteem requires actively encouraging your child's independence. This doesn't mean abandoning them to fend for themselves; it means gradually empowering them to take on age-appropriate responsibilities and challenges. Let them make choices, even small ones, and allow them to experience the natural consequences of their decisions. This fosters a sense of agency and competence, vital ingredients in building self-esteem. For instance, letting them choose their own clothes (within reason), allowing them to help with chores, or encouraging them to participate in extracurricular activities, all contribute to this sense of autonomy. Celebrate their efforts, even if the outcome isn't perfect. Focus on the process of learning and growth, not just the end result.

Another crucial aspect is celebrating effort over outcome. In our achievement-oriented culture, we often inadvertently place undue emphasis on results. While accomplishments should be acknowledged and celebrated, it's equally important – perhaps even more so – to recognize and praise the effort and perseverance involved. A child who consistently puts forth their best effort will develop a strong sense of self-efficacy, believing in their ability to overcome obstacles. If they don't achieve a desired outcome,
acknowledge their hard work and encourage them to learn from the experience. For example, if they participate in a sports competition and don't win, praise their dedication to training and their sportsmanship. Frame setbacks as learning opportunities, emphasizing the valuable lessons gained, not just the final score.

Encouraging healthy risk-taking is also essential. Children need to feel safe to step outside their comfort zones, to try new things, and to experience failure without fear of ridicule or punishment. This doesn't mean encouraging reckless behavior; it means providing a supportive environment where they feel comfortable taking calculated risks and learning from their mistakes. This might involve encouraging them to try out for a school play, join a sports team, or learn a new instrument. The key is to emphasize the learning process and the development of new skills, even if the initial attempts are less than perfect.

Furthermore, cultivating empathy and compassion plays a critical role in building self-esteem. Children who understand and value the feelings of others are better equipped to navigate social situations and build positive relationships. Encourage acts of kindness and service, whether it's volunteering at a local charity or simply helping a sibling with a task. These acts foster a sense of purpose and belonging, contributing significantly to a child's self-worth. Discuss social issues and encourage them to think critically about the world around them. Empower them to make a positive impact, however small.

Equally important is fostering a child's unique talents and interests. Every child has something they excel at, whether it's art, music, sports, or academics. Identifying and nurturing these talents allows them to experience a sense of accomplishment and self-confidence. Provide opportunities for them to explore their interests and develop their skills.

This might involve enrolling them in classes, providing access to resources, or simply spending quality time engaging in activities they enjoy. The goal is not to create child prodigies, but to allow them to discover their passions and build self-esteem through mastery of a skill.

Another crucial element is teaching children effective communication skills. This encompasses both expressing their needs and listening attentively to others. Encourage them to articulate their feelings and perspectives, even when it's challenging. Teach them assertive communication techniques, helping them to express their needs and opinions respectfully while setting boundaries. Conversely, teach them the importance of active listening, empathizing with others' viewpoints. This skill is crucial not only for building positive relationships but also for fostering self-advocacy and self-confidence. A child who can effectively communicate their needs is more likely to feel empowered and in control of their life.

Finally, remember that self-esteem is not a static quality; it fluctuates throughout life. There will be times when your child's self-esteem is high and times when it dips. The key is to provide consistent, unwavering support during both the highs and lows. Be patient, understanding, and empathetic.

Help them to identify their strengths and weaknesses, to celebrate their successes, and to learn from their setbacks. Ultimately, fostering self-esteem is about helping your child develop a strong sense of self, a belief in their own worth, and the resilience to navigate life's inevitable challenges with confidence and grace. This is an ongoing process, a testament to the enduring power of love, understanding, and unwavering support. It's an investment that pays dividends far beyond childhood, shaping the individual your child becomes and the life they lead. The rewards, in terms of their emotional well-being and life success, are immeasurable.

Remember that this isn't merely about raising a resilient child; it's about raising a confident, compassionate, and fulfilled human being.

Promoting Emotional Regulation

Building a child's resilience requires more than simply teaching them how to cope; it demands equipping them with the tools to manage their emotional landscape. Emotional regulation, the ability to understand and manage one's feelings, is the cornerstone of resilience. A child who can effectively identify, express, and navigate their emotions is better prepared to handle life's inevitable stressors. This isn't about suppressing feelings; rather, it's about developing a healthy relationship with them, viewing them not as enemies to be conquered, but as valuable sources of information about their internal world.

One of the first steps in promoting emotional regulation is fostering emotional literacy. This involves helping your child develop a rich vocabulary for their feelings. Instead of simply saying "I'm sad," encourage them to explore the nuances of their emotions. Are they disappointed, heartbroken, lonely, or frustrated? The more precise their language, the better they can understand and communicate their inner state. Introduce them to emotion charts, books, or even games that explore a wide range of feelings, helping them build a comprehensive understanding of the emotional spectrum.

This process begins early in childhood. Even toddlers can learn to identify basic emotions like happy, sad, and angry. Use simple language, point to pictures, and engage them in role-playing scenarios to illustrate different emotional states. As they grow older, delve into more complex emotions, such as jealousy, guilt, or pride. Openly discuss your own feelings, modeling healthy emotional expression and regulation for them. Let them witness you navigating

challenging emotions in a constructive way, showing them that it's okay to feel a wide range of emotions, and that even adults struggle to regulate their emotions at times. This creates a safe space for them to share their feelings without fear of judgment or criticism.

Remember to validate their feelings, regardless of how insignificant they might seem to you. Telling a child that their feelings are "silly" or "over the top" invalidates their experience and undermines their trust in you. Instead, acknowledge their emotions, even if you don't entirely understand them. You might say, "It sounds like you're feeling really angry about that," or "I can see that you're feeling really sad." This simple act of validation helps them feel heard and understood, fostering a sense of security and trust.

Once children can identify their emotions, the next step involves teaching them strategies for managing them. This might involve deep breathing exercises, mindfulness techniques, or even physical activities like running or playing. Introduce these strategies gradually, starting with simple techniques and gradually building up to more complex ones. For younger children, simple counting exercises can be effective in calming them down during moments of frustration. Older children can benefit from mindfulness apps or guided meditation exercises.

Experiment with different approaches to find what works best for your child. Consider creating a calm-down corner in their room, a designated space where they can retreat to when they feel overwhelmed.

The importance of physical activity cannot be overstated. Exercise acts as a natural mood booster, releasing endorphins that combat stress and improve mood. Regular physical activity is not only beneficial for physical health but also plays a crucial role in emotional well-being. Encourage your child to engage in activities they enjoy, whether it's dancing, swimming, cycling, or team sports. This provides an outlet for pent-up energy and emotions. And remember, even a short burst of activity, such as a quick walk or a game of catch, can make a significant difference.

Beyond physical activities, creative outlets such as drawing, painting, writing, or playing music can be invaluable tools for emotional expression and regulation. These activities provide a safe space for children to express themselves without words, processing their feelings in a healthy and creative way. Encourage them to explore their creativity, providing them with the resources and support they need to express themselves artistically.

Teaching problem-solving skills is another crucial aspect of promoting emotional regulation. When children encounter challenging situations, they need the tools to navigate them effectively. This involves teaching them to identify the problem, brainstorm potential solutions, and evaluate the consequences of each solution. Role-playing exercises can be incredibly helpful in this process, allowing children to practice their problem-solving skills in a safe and controlled environment. Frame these exercises as opportunities for them to learn and grow, emphasizing that even making mistakes is part of the learning process.

Establishing consistent routines and boundaries is also essential for emotional well-being. Predictability provides a sense of security and stability, which helps children feel safe and in control. Children thrive on routines, and the lack of consistent boundaries can often lead to frustration, anxiety, and a decrease in self-regulation. Clear, consistent expectations, paired with supportive guidance, empower children. They learn to anticipate and navigate situations with a greater sense of confidence and self-assurance,
promoting a sense of calm and control that fosters emotional resilience. Avoid chaotic environments and aim for structure and predictability in their daily lives.

Communication remains the lifeblood of healthy parent-child relationships and successful emotional regulation. This necessitates open and honest dialogues. Establish a safe space for your child to express their feelings without fear of judgment or criticism. Active listening is paramount – truly hearing what your child is saying, rather than simply waiting for your turn to speak. Reflect their emotions back to them, demonstrating your understanding. Engage in regular family conversations, encouraging open dialogue about everyday experiences and feelings. This builds a strong foundation of trust and understanding, creating an environment where your child feels comfortable sharing their vulnerabilities.

Remember that emotional regulation is a skill that develops over time. It's not something that can be taught overnight. Be patient and supportive, providing your child with the tools and resources they need to develop these essential skills. Celebrate their successes, no matter how small, and provide encouragement when they face setbacks. Acknowledge that learning emotional regulation is an ongoing process, and that there will be times when they struggle. This journey is as much about your own emotional regulation and self- awareness as it is about your child's. By modeling healthy emotional responses and providing consistent support, you can help your child develop the emotional resilience they need to thrive. This is an investment in their present well-being and their future success. It's about nurturing not just their ability to cope with challenges, but also their capacity for joy, empathy, and lasting fulfillment. This holistic approach fosters not just resilience, but a well-rounded, emotionally intelligent individual, capable of navigating life's complexities with grace and confidence. The strength of their emotional foundation will serve them well long after childhood years.

Encouraging Problem Solving Skills

Building a child's resilience isn't solely about shielding them from hardship; it's about empowering them to navigate challenges independently. A crucial element of this empowerment lies in fostering their problem-solving skills. This isn't about turning children into miniature strategists overnight, but rather about cultivating a mindset that approaches obstacles with curiosity and resourcefulness, not fear or avoidance.

The journey begins early. Even toddlers grapple with simple problems: a toy that's out of reach, a spilled cup of milk, a puzzle piece that refuses to fit. These seemingly minor incidents are fertile ground for nurturing problem-solving skills. Instead of immediately rushing in to fix the issue, observe your child's attempts. Are they experimenting? Are they frustrated? Your response should be tailored to their developmental stage. With a toddler, gentle guidance is key.

You might offer a suggestion, such as, "Hmm, maybe you could try using that spoon to reach the toy," or, "Let's see if we can use a cloth to wipe up the milk." The goal isn't to solve the problem for them, but to help them find a solution, fostering their own sense of agency and accomplishment.

As children grow, the complexity of their challenges increases. A missed homework assignment, a conflict with a friend, or a difficult math problem demand more sophisticated problem-solving strategies. Here, the focus shifts from direct intervention to facilitating their own problem-solving process. This involves asking open-ended questions that encourage critical thinking. Instead of saying, "Why didn't you finish your homework?" try, "What happened that made it hard to finish your homework tonight?" Or, instead of jumping in to mediate a disagreement, ask, "Can you two tell me what happened?

Let's see if we can find a way to solve this together."

This approach nurtures several essential skills. Firstly, it fosters self-reflection. By encouraging children to articulate their thoughts and feelings, you're helping them develop metacognitive abilities—the capacity to think about their own thinking. This is crucial for effective problem-solving. They begin to understand their strengths and weaknesses, their emotional responses to challenges, and the impact of their choices.

Secondly, it promotes creative thinking. When children are encouraged to find their own solutions, they are less likely to rely on pre-programmed responses or to accept limitations without question. They learn to explore multiple perspectives, consider different options, and develop creative solutions tailored to the specific problem at hand. This fosters resilience in the face of unexpected challenges – the very essence of adaptability.

Thirdly, it builds confidence. Each successful problem solved, no matter how small, reinforces their belief in their ability to overcome challenges. This sense of self-efficacy is a powerful antidote to learned helplessness, the feeling that their efforts are futile. It fosters a growth mindset, a belief that abilities can be developed through dedication and hard work. This is paramount not only for academic success but for navigating the complexities of life itself.

Remember, the process is as important as the outcome. It's perfectly acceptable for children to make mistakes. Indeed, mistakes are invaluable learning opportunities. Instead of criticizing errors, approach them as chances to learn and improve. Ask questions like, "What did you learn from that experience?" or "What could you try differently next time?" This helps them analyze their approach, identify areas for improvement, and develop a more effective strategy for future challenges.

The cultivation of problem-solving skills extends beyond academics and social situations. It permeates all aspects of their lives, influencing their decision-making processes, their adaptability to change, and their overall sense of self-reliance. A resilient child is not one who never faces

difficulties, but one who approaches difficulties with a proactive, resourceful spirit. They understand that setbacks are inevitable, but they also know they possess the skills to navigate them successfully.

Incorporate problem-solving into everyday routines. Engage them in household tasks that require decision-making and problem-solving. For example, let them help plan a meal, choosing recipes and figuring out the necessary ingredients and steps. Or, involve them in organizing a family outing, requiring them to consider logistics, budget, and preferences.

These real-world scenarios offer valuable learning opportunities and demonstrate the practical application of problem-solving skills.

Furthermore, provide opportunities for collaborative problem-solving. Group projects, team sports, and even playing board games together can teach children the value of teamwork, negotiation, and compromise. These experiences not only build problem-solving skills but also enhance social and emotional intelligence. They learn to work effectively with others, to understand different perspectives, and to resolve conflicts constructively.

Role-playing scenarios can also be incredibly beneficial. Present them with hypothetical problems, encouraging them to think creatively and devise solutions. These exercises can range from simple scenarios, such as what to do if they lose a favorite toy, to more complex ones, such as how to handle bullying or peer pressure. The key is to create a safe space where children feel comfortable exploring different options without fear of judgment.

It's important to note that the development of problem-solving skills is a gradual process. It requires patience, consistency, and a supportive environment where children feel safe to take risks, make mistakes, and learn from their experiences. Celebrate their efforts, acknowledge their progress, and offer encouragement when they face setbacks.

Your role is not to solve their problems for them, but to empower them to find their own solutions, fostering their independence, self-reliance, and ultimately, their resilience.

The benefits extend far beyond childhood. Strong problem-solving skills are essential for success in all areas of life, from academic pursuits and career development to personal relationships and navigating life's inevitable challenges. By equipping your child with these vital skills, you're not only building their resilience but investing in their future happiness and well-being. Remember that fostering

resilience is a holistic endeavor; it's about nurturing their emotional intelligence, their problem-solving abilities, and their overall sense of self-efficacy. This integrated approach ensures they are not just equipped to handle adversity but also thrive in the face of it. The resilience you cultivate will be a gift that keeps on giving, enriching their lives long after they leave the nest.

The journey of fostering resilience is a continuous one, a partnership between parent and child. It's a journey filled with challenges, setbacks, and triumphs, but the reward – a child equipped to face life's complexities with confidence and grace – is immeasurable. The 'hidden crack' we strive to avoid is not just about preventing problems; it's about empowering our children to navigate them, to emerge

stronger, wiser, and more resilient than ever before. The skills you instill today will serve them well, not only in overcoming challenges but in embracing life's opportunities with courage and a sense of self-belief that stems from knowing they possess the tools to shape their own destiny.

The process demands patience, understanding, and a commitment to nurturing not just their abilities but their spirit, their innate capacity for growth and resilience. It's an investment in their future, a future brimming with possibilities, a future where they are not merely survivors, but confident, resourceful, and resilient individuals capable of achieving their dreams.

Building Independence

The seeds of resilience are sown not in a bubble wrap existence, free from the prick of disappointment or the sting of failure, but in the fertile ground of independence. A child who learns to tie their own shoelaces, pack their own lunch, or navigate the complexities of a playground without constant parental intervention is not merely mastering a task; they are building a foundation of self-reliance that will serve them well throughout their lives. This isn't about abandoning our children to fend for themselves; it's about carefully guiding them toward self-sufficiency, empowering them to tackle challenges with confidence and resourcefulness.

Think of it like learning to ride a bike. We don't simply strap a helmet on our child and push them off a cliff, hoping for the best. Instead, we start with small steps: holding onto the bike seat, then letting go for a few seconds, then longer intervals, providing support and encouragement along the way. Gradually, as their balance improves and their confidence grows, we step back, allowing them to experience the exhilaration of independent movement.

Falling is part of the process, of course, but each fall becomes a lesson in perseverance, a step closer to mastering the skill. The same principle applies to fostering independence in other areas of a child's life.

Begin small. Don't overwhelm your child with monumental tasks. Instead, break down complex activities into manageable steps. Instead of expecting your child to clean their entire room at once, start with just one drawer. Instead of assigning the entire laundry chore, begin with folding a single load of towels. Praise their efforts, focusing on their progress rather than perfection. A small victory, like successfully putting away their toys, should be celebrated as a significant achievement, building their self-esteem and encouraging them to tackle more challenging tasks in the future.

As children grow, gradually increase the level of independence you allow them. A six-year-old might need more guidance than a ten-year-old when it comes to managing their time or making responsible choices. Observe their abilities and adapt your approach accordingly. Allow them to make age-appropriate decisions, even if it means making the occasional mistake. Learning from mistakes is a vital part of the process; it teaches them valuable lessons about problem-solving and taking responsibility for their actions.

The temptation to rescue our children from every challenge can be overwhelming, particularly when we see them struggling. But intervening too quickly can undermine their developing sense of self-reliance. Instead, consider offering guidance and support without taking over. Ask questions that encourage them to think critically and solve problems on their own. For example, if your child is struggling with a difficult homework assignment, don't simply do it for them.

Instead, ask them what part they are finding challenging, what strategies they have already tried, and what resources they might utilize to overcome the obstacle. This approach cultivates their problem-solving abilities, fostering a sense of accomplishment and boosting their confidence.

This process extends beyond academic tasks. Encourage your children to participate in household chores that are appropriate for their age and abilities. Setting the table, washing dishes, tidying up their rooms – these are not merely chores; they are opportunities to develop responsibility and contribute to the family unit. This sense of

contribution is vital for fostering a child's self-esteem and sense of belonging. It teaches them that they are valued members of the family and that their efforts make a difference.

Another significant aspect of building independence is fostering their decision-making skills. Start by providing choices within reasonable limits. Instead of dictating what they wear, offer them a selection of outfits. Allow them to choose their own books to read, their favorite snacks, or the activities they want to pursue after school. These seemingly small choices are powerful tools for cultivating their autonomy and preparing them for more complex decision-making in the future.

However, fostering independence is not synonymous with complete freedom. Establishing clear boundaries and expectations is essential. Children need to know what is expected of them, what behaviors are acceptable and unacceptable. Consistency in enforcing these boundaries is critical for creating a sense of security and stability, giving them a framework within which they can explore their independence. Inconsistency can lead to confusion and anxiety, undermining their sense of safety and hindering their development of self-reliance.

The balance between freedom and responsibility is a delicate one. It's about allowing children to make choices, to learn from their mistakes, and to grow in confidence, all while ensuring their safety and well-being. This is not a race to be won but a journey to be undertaken together, a partnership between parent and child. It's about nurturing their innate capabilities, fostering their self-belief, and empowering them to become confident, independent, and resilient individuals, ready to face the challenges and opportunities that life throws their way. Remember, the goal is not to produce perfect children, but rather to raise capable, responsible, and well-adjusted adults.

The journey towards independence involves inevitable setbacks. There will be moments of frustration, moments when your child struggles or makes mistakes. These are opportunities for learning and growth, not reasons for discouragement. Offer your unwavering support, reminding them of their strengths, and guiding them through their difficulties. Celebrate their successes, no matter how small. Each step forward, each obstacle overcome, strengthens their sense of self-efficacy and reinforces their belief in their own abilities.

A resilient child is not a child who avoids challenges; it's a child who confronts them with courage and resourcefulness.

It is a child who possesses the independence to navigate difficulties, to seek solutions, and to learn from their experiences. Independence is not a destination but a

continuous process of growth and development, a journey that requires patience, understanding, and a steadfast commitment from both parent and child. It is an investment in their future, a future where they are not merely passive recipients of life's events, but active participants, shaping their own destinies with confidence and grace. Beyond the Cracks of Carewe seek to avoid is not just about shielding our

children from hardship; it's about empowering them to overcome it, to emerge stronger and more resilient than ever before. The tools of independence are the bedrock upon which we build their resilient spirit.

The cultivation of independence extends beyond the home; it encompasses the broader social environment. Encourage your child to participate in extracurricular activities, fostering their social skills and allowing them to navigate social dynamics independently. This might involve joining a sports team, participating in a club, or engaging in community service. These experiences provide opportunities for them to build relationships, learn teamwork, and develop their communication skills, all essential components of a resilient and well-adjusted personality.

Encourage problem-solving through play. Provide your child with open-ended toys and activities that encourage creativity and imaginative problem-solving. Building blocks, puzzles, and art supplies are excellent tools for fostering their cognitive skills and their ability to think critically and creatively. Engage in activities that require collaborative problem-solving, such as board games or building projects. These activities help them learn to work together, negotiate, and compromise, skills that are valuable in all aspects of life.

Observe your child's interests and passions, and nurture their development in those areas. Providing opportunities for them to explore their talents and interests builds confidence and self-esteem, further strengthening their sense of independence and resilience. Whether it's music, art, sports, or academics, supporting their pursuits fosters a sense of purpose and accomplishment, equipping them with skills and experiences that contribute to their overall well-being.

Finally, remember that fostering independence is a marathon, not a sprint. There will be moments of doubt, moments when you question your approach, moments when your child struggles. But the rewards of raising a confident, independent, and resilient child far outweigh the challenges.

Your unwavering support, guidance, and belief in your child's abilities will lay the foundation for a life filled with purpose, accomplishment, and joy. The resilience you cultivate today will serve them well not only in overcoming challenges but in embracing opportunities with courage and self-belief, knowing they possess the tools to navigate life's complexities and shape their own destiny. This is the ultimate gift of parenthood, a gift that transcends material possessions and provides a lasting legacy of strength and empowerment.

SEVEN
STRENGTHENING FAMILY BONDS

The foundation of a child's well-being rests not just on individual interactions with parents, but on the strength and health of the entire family unit. A strong family bond acts as a buffer against the challenges of life, providing a safe haven where children feel loved, accepted, and supported. This sense of belonging is paramount; it's the bedrock upon which self-esteem, resilience, and emotional intelligence are built. Without it, even the most well-intentioned parenting efforts can fall short. Think of a tree – the roots, representing the family, must be strong to support the branches (the individual child) that reach for the sky. If the roots are weak or damaged, the tree, despite having strong branches, is vulnerable to storms.

Strengthening family bonds isn't about grand gestures or elaborate vacations; it's about the consistent, small actions that build a culture of connection and mutual respect. It starts with open and honest communication. This doesn't mean every conversation needs to be a deep philosophical debate, but rather a commitment to creating a space where everyone feels comfortable expressing their thoughts and feelings without fear of judgment. This requires active listening—truly hearing what your children are saying, both verbally and nonverbally. Put down your phone, make eye contact, and show genuine interest in their experiences, even the seemingly insignificant ones. Ask open-ended questions ("Tell me about your day") rather than closed ones ("Did you have a good day?"), encouraging detailed responses and deeper engagement.

Family dinners, a seemingly mundane ritual, can be a powerful tool for connection. Turning off screens and engaging in conversation around the dinner table creates a shared experience and fosters a sense of togetherness. These shared meals aren't just about nourishment; they're about sharing stories, laughing together, and connecting over everyday events. It's a time to create memories and strengthen family bonds. If your family is particularly busy, even 15 minutes of dedicated family time, free from distractions, can make a significant difference. Shared responsibilities are another cornerstone of a strong family unit. Assigning age-appropriate chores not only teaches children valuable life skills but also instills a sense of contribution and belonging. This fosters a sense of teamwork, where everyone contributes to the smooth

functioning of the household. It's not about creating a miniature factory, but about creating a sense of shared responsibility and collaborative effort. Involving children in decision-making processes, even concerning smaller household matters, empowers them and fosters a sense of ownership and belonging.

Family rituals and traditions are the glue that binds a family together. Whether it's a weekly game night, a monthly family outing, or annual traditions passed down through generations, these shared experiences create lasting memories and a strong sense of identity. These traditions don't have to be extravagant or expensive; they could be as simple as reading a bedtime story together every night or baking cookies on a Sunday afternoon. The key is consistency and the shared enjoyment of the experience.

These traditions provide a sense of predictability and stability, particularly beneficial during periods of stress or uncertainty.

Beyond the everyday rituals, consider engaging in activities that encourage collaboration and teamwork. A family project, like building a birdhouse or planting a garden, can be both fun and rewarding, fostering a sense of shared accomplishment. Participating in community events, volunteering together, or simply spending time outdoors as a family can strengthen bonds and create shared experiences.

Even a simple walk in the park, engaging in conversation, can be a powerful way to connect. Crucially, fostering a strong family unit requires self- awareness and self-care on the part of the parents. Burnout, stress, and neglecting your own well-being inevitably negatively impact your ability to be present and engaged with your children. Taking time for yourself, engaging in activities you enjoy, and prioritizing your own mental and physical health isn't selfish; it's essential for effective parenting. A parent who is well-rested, emotionally balanced, and engaged in their own life is better equipped to nurture and support their children.

This also extends to seeking support when needed. Parenting is challenging, and there's no shame in admitting that you need help. Reaching out to family, friends, support groups, or professionals when struggling isn't a sign of weakness but of strength. Recognizing your limitations and seeking
assistance demonstrates a commitment to your own well-being and that of your family. There are numerous support networks available, from online forums to in-person groups, where parents can connect with others facing similar challenges and gain valuable insights and support.

Remember, building strong family bonds is an ongoing process, not a destination. It requires consistent effort, patience, and a commitment to creating a nurturing and supportive environment. There will be ups and downs, challenges and triumphs, but the investment in strengthening these bonds is an investment in the well-being of each family member and the long-term happiness and success of your children. It's about cultivating a culture of love, respect, and connection that will resonate throughout your children's lives, shaping their capacity for healthy relationships and fostering their emotional resilience. And ultimately, it's about building a legacy of love, a strong family tree with deep roots that can weather any storm. The effort you invest today will bear fruit for generations to come, creating a ripple effect of positivity and well-being within your family and beyond. Embrace the journey, celebrate the small victories, and remember that even amidst challenges, the bond you share as a family is a powerful force. This commitment to connection is the most valuable gift you can give your children.

Effective Family Communication

The previous chapter emphasized the crucial role of the family unit as a foundation for a child's well-being. We explored the analogy of a tree, where the strength of the roots (family bonds) directly impacts the resilience of the branches (individual children). Now, let's delve into the practical application of strengthening these roots through effective family communication. Building strong, healthy communication isn't about magical solutions or quick fixes; it's about consistent, conscious effort, a cultivation of skills and understanding within the family dynamic. It's a continuous process of learning and adapting, much like nurturing a garden. Weeding out negativity, planting seeds of empathy, and regularly tending to the emotional landscape of the family are key.

Effective family communication begins with actively listening. This isn't merely hearing the words spoken; it's truly absorbing the message, understanding the emotions behind it, and responding thoughtfully. Too often, we fall into the trap of thinking about our response while someone else is speaking, interrupting the flow of genuine connection. Truly listening involves putting aside distractions – turning off the television, silencing our phones, and giving the speaker our undivided attention. It means observing
nonverbal cues – body language, tone of voice, facial expressions – to gain a complete understanding of what's being conveyed.

Furthermore, effective listening necessitates empathy. Stepping into another person's shoes, acknowledging their feelings, and validating their experiences are paramount. A simple statement like, "I understand you're feeling frustrated," can go a long way in diffusing conflict and fostering a sense of understanding. Even if you don't agree with the speaker's perspective, acknowledging their feelings demonstrates respect and creates a safe space for open dialogue. Avoid interrupting with your own opinions or experiences before fully grasping their point of view. The aim is to create a space where every family member feels heard and understood, not judged or dismissed.

Open and honest communication is another cornerstone of a healthy family dynamic. Creating a culture where every family member feels comfortable expressing their thoughts and feelings, both positive and negative, is essential. This requires establishing clear boundaries and ground rules for respectful communication. It's crucial to teach children that it's okay to disagree, but it's equally important to do so respectfully. Shouting matches and personal attacks should be discouraged, replaced with calm, measured discussions.

Family meetings, even informal ones, can provide a structured environment for discussing concerns, resolving conflicts, and making decisions as a unit. However, open communication extends beyond simply airing grievances. It also involves expressing appreciation and affection. Regularly expressing gratitude for each other's contributions, celebrating successes both big and small, and actively showing love and support creates a positive emotional climate within the family. Small gestures like a heartfelt "thank you," a warm hug, or a simple "I love you" can significantly strengthen family bonds. These seemingly insignificant acts of affection cumulate over time, building a foundation of trust and security. Moreover, taking the time to acknowledge individual achievements, however minor they may seem, fosters self-esteem and encourages a sense of accomplishment within each family member.

Beyond verbal communication, nonverbal cues play a vital role in effective family interaction. Body language, tone of voice, and even facial expressions transmit powerful messages that can either strengthen or damage relationships.

A warm smile, a gentle touch, or attentive eye contact can convey love and support, while a cold stare, a dismissive tone, or crossed arms can communicate disinterest or disapproval. Being mindful of our nonverbal communication, ensuring it aligns with our verbal messages, contributes significantly to clear and effective interactions. Teaching children to recognize and interpret nonverbal cues also equips them with crucial social skills, improving their ability to navigate social situations.

Regular family meals provide an excellent opportunity for fostering communication. These are not just times for consuming food; they are valuable opportunities for connection, conversation, and shared experiences. The act of sitting together, engaging in meaningful dialogue, and sharing stories strengthens family bonds. These meals don't need to be elaborate affairs; a simple, shared meal can be enough to create a warm and welcoming atmosphere. The shared experience of preparing and enjoying food provides a context for connecting and communicating, creating cherished memories along the way. Making these meals a consistent part of the family routine cultivates a sense of community and shared identity.

Conflict is inevitable in any family, but how conflicts are managed defines the health of communication and family dynamics. Rather than avoiding conflict, families should learn to navigate disagreements constructively. This involves teaching children healthy conflict resolution skills such as active listening, empathy, and compromise. It also requires parents to model healthy conflict management techniques. Showing children how to express their anger and frustration without resorting to aggression or personal attacks is vital.

Encouraging them to articulate their feelings and needs clearly, while respectfully listening to the perspective of others, equips them with crucial life skills. When conflicts arise, parents should act as facilitators, guiding the children through the process of finding solutions that are mutually acceptable.

Technology, while beneficial in many aspects, can impede effective family communication if not managed carefully. Excessive screen time can lead to isolation, reduced face-to-face interaction, and diminished opportunities for meaningful conversations. Establishing clear guidelines for screen time, encouraging alternative activities such as family games, reading together, or engaging in outdoor activities, can help to balance technology's role in the family. Creating screen-free zones and times, such as during mealtimes or before bedtime, can help prioritize face-to-face interaction and foster closer relationships. This conscious effort to minimize technology's dominance allows for more meaningful interactions, strengthening family bonds and improving communication.

Moreover, creating opportunities for shared experiences beyond the daily routine strengthens family communication. Engaging in activities such as family outings, vacations, or volunteering together creates shared memories and fosters a sense of unity. These experiences provide a context for communication and strengthen family bonds. The shared challenges and triumphs create opportunities for teamwork, problem-solving, and mutual support, enhancing trust and understanding among family members. These experiences can be simple – a family walk, a bike ride, or even a movie night – but the shared activity is what truly matters.

Finally, prioritizing quality time is essential for strengthening family communication. This means scheduling dedicated time for family activities, even amidst busy schedules. This could be as simple as having a family game night, reading together before bedtime, or engaging in a shared hobby. This focused time creates opportunities for meaningful connection, strengthens family bonds, and enhances communication. Even small blocks of focused time can be far more beneficial than large stretches of diffused attention. The consistent commitment to these shared moments demonstrates the importance of family and enhances mutual understanding and strengthens the relationships. The investment in quality time is an investment in the emotional well-being of every family member and is crucial to building a strong, loving, and communicative family unit. Remember, effective communication is an ongoing journey, not a destination.

Consistent effort, patience, and a commitment to fostering open dialogue will strengthen family bonds and contribute significantly to the overall well-being of each family member.

EIGHT

SHARED RESPONSIBILITIES AND TEAMWORK

Building upon the foundation of strong communication, the next crucial element in fostering a thriving family unit is the establishment of shared responsibilities and teamwork. This isn't merely about dividing chores; it's about cultivating a sense of collective ownership and mutual support. It's about teaching children the value of contribution, fostering a sense of belonging, and building resilience in the face of life's inevitable challenges. Think of it as a finely tuned orchestra, where each member plays their part, contributing to the harmonious whole. A family that works together, thrives together.

The concept of shared responsibility begins in the early years. Even toddlers can contribute to household tasks, albeit in age-appropriate ways. Putting away toys, helping to set the table, or assisting with simple gardening tasks instills a sense of purpose and accomplishment. As children grow, their contributions should increase in complexity and responsibility. This gradual progression teaches them valuable life skills, fostering a sense of independence and self-reliance. Imagine a family where the older sibling helps the younger with homework, or where everyone contributes to meal preparation, creating a collaborative atmosphere filled with shared laughter and accomplishment.

The key to successful shared responsibility lies in clear communication and realistic expectations. Parents should explain the importance of each task, emphasizing its contribution to the overall well-being of the family. It's not about burdening children with chores; it's about empowering them to become contributing members of the household. A family meeting, perhaps a weekly event, can serve as a forum for discussing household tasks, delegating responsibilities, and celebrating successes. This open dialogue ensures that everyone feels heard and valued, promoting a sense of fairness and cooperation. A chore chart, visually representing each person's contributions, can further enhance this collaborative approach.

The allocation of responsibilities should take into account each family member's age, abilities, and interests. Avoid assigning tasks that are overly challenging or tedious.

Instead, focus on finding tasks that are age-appropriate and engaging, allowing children to experience a sense of pride in their contributions. For instance, a young child might enjoy watering plants, while an older child might be responsible for grocery shopping or meal planning. Flexibility is paramount; adjust responsibilities as children grow and their capabilities evolve. Regularly review and adjust the chore distribution to ensure it remains fair and manageable.

Beyond the realm of household chores, shared responsibilities extend to other areas of family life. Decision-making, problem-solving, and conflict resolution should involve every family member, fostering a sense of collective ownership and shared responsibility. Involve children in age-appropriate decision-making processes, such as planning family outings or choosing a movie to watch together. This empowers them to contribute their ideas and perspectives, strengthening family bonds and fostering a sense of belonging. Through collaborative problem-solving, children learn valuable skills in negotiation, compromise, and critical thinking. The family unit becomes a training ground for navigating the complexities of interpersonal relationships and resolving conflicts constructively.

Teamwork within the family isn't merely about dividing labor; it's about cultivating a shared sense of purpose and mutual support. It's about celebrating each other's successes and offering support during challenging times. Family traditions, rituals, and shared activities create a sense of unity and belonging, strengthening family bonds and enhancing communication. Family meals, game nights, or regular outings together foster positive interactions and shared experiences. These moments create lasting memories and strengthen the emotional fabric of the family.

Regular family meetings offer a valuable platform for open communication, fostering teamwork and shared responsibility. These meetings provide a safe space for family members to express their concerns, share their ideas, and collaboratively solve problems. They promote a sense of shared ownership and contribute to a more harmonious family dynamic. In addition to addressing household chores, these meetings can also be used to discuss family goals, plan events, and share updates on individual achievements and challenges.

When children witness their parents working collaboratively and supporting each other, they learn valuable lessons about teamwork and mutual respect. Parents should model these behaviors, demonstrating how to effectively communicate, negotiate compromises, and support each other during
challenging times. This modeling establishes a foundation for healthy relationships and contributes to the overall well-being of the family. When disagreements arise, parents should resolve them constructively, demonstrating empathy, understanding, and a willingness to find common ground.

However, it's essential to acknowledge that cultivating shared responsibility and teamwork within the family is an ongoing process, not a destination. There will be challenges, disagreements, and moments of frustration. The key is to persevere, adapt to changing circumstances, and maintain
open communication. Regularly evaluate the effectiveness of the system, adjusting responsibilities and approaches as needed. Celebrate successes, learn from setbacks, and consistently reinforce the importance of mutual support and collaboration.

The benefits of shared responsibility and teamwork extend far beyond the confines of the home. Children who learn to work collaboratively within their families develop essential social skills that serve them well throughout their lives. They learn to cooperate, compromise, and resolve conflicts effectively, skills that are invaluable in their academic pursuits, social interactions, and future relationships. They also develop a strong sense of self-esteem and confidence, knowing that they are valued members of a supportive team.

A family that works together, not only manages its affairs more efficiently but builds strong bonds that endure the challenges of life. This cohesive unit becomes a source of strength and support, helping each member navigate the complexities of life with greater resilience and grace.

Moreover, the experience of shared responsibility fosters a sense of community and belonging. Children understand that they are integral parts of a larger system, their contributions mattering and impacting the whole. This knowledge instills a sense of purpose and belonging, contributing to their emotional well-being and overall development. A child who feels valued and needed is more likely to develop a strong sense of self-worth and a positive self-image. This contributes significantly to their emotional resilience and their ability to navigate the inevitable challenges of life.

Therefore, the establishment of shared responsibilities and teamwork within the family unit is not merely a practical solution for managing household tasks; it is a vital component in fostering a healthy, supportive, and nurturing environment where children can thrive. It's about building a strong foundation for future success, equipping children with life skills and emotional resilience, ultimately shaping them into well-adjusted, contributing members of society. The family that functions as a unified team, where every member plays their part, is a family that is well-positioned to face the future with confidence, resilience, and a shared sense of purpose. It's a testament to the power of collective effort, the enduring strength of family bonds, and the transformative potential of a truly collaborative approach to family life.

This collaborative spirit, nurtured from the earliest years, will serve as a guiding principle throughout a child's life, informing their relationships, influencing their decisions, and shaping their capacity for empathy and mutual support. The investment in fostering shared responsibility and teamwork within the family is an investment in the future, an investment in the well-being of each family member, and an investment in the strength and resilience of the family unit as a whole.

Family Rituals and Traditions

Building upon the foundation of shared responsibility and teamwork, we now turn to the powerful role of family rituals and traditions in strengthening the family unit. These aren't merely sentimental gestures; they are the bedrock upon which lasting bonds are built, a source of comfort and continuity in a world that often feels chaotic and unpredictable. Family rituals are the invisible threads that weave together the tapestry of family life, creating a sense of belonging, shared identity, and emotional security. They provide a sense of normalcy and predictability, particularly crucial during times of stress or transition.

Think about it: the nightly bedtime story, the Sunday morning pancake breakfast, the annual family vacation, the holiday celebrations replete with cherished customs – these seemingly small moments accumulate over time, becoming potent symbols of connection and love. They are the shared experiences that forge lasting memories, shaping a child's understanding of family, belonging, and their place within the world. These rituals are not just about the activities themselves; they are about the consistent presence, the shared focus, and the unspoken message they convey: "You are loved, you are important, you belong here."

The benefits extend far beyond simple sentimentality.

Research consistently shows that families with strong rituals and traditions exhibit higher levels of emotional well-being, stronger communication, and increased resilience. Children who participate in regular family rituals are often better equipped to handle stress, demonstrate greater self-esteem, and display improved social skills. These rituals provide a safe haven, a predictable structure within which children can explore their emotions and develop a sense of identity. The consistent repetition reinforces a sense of security and belonging, vital for a child's healthy development.

Consider the power of a simple bedtime routine. It's more than just brushing teeth and getting into pajamas. The nightly story, the quiet conversation, the shared moment of physical affection – these are opportunities to connect, to nurture, and to reinforce the bond between parent and child. This consistent ritual offers predictability in a child's world, helping them to wind down and prepare for sleep. It's a predictable ending to a potentially unpredictable day, providing a sense of security and control.

Similarly, family meals offer invaluable opportunities for connection and communication. It's a time to share stories, discuss the day's events, and simply be together. The shared meal itself becomes a symbolic act, a ritual that underscores the importance of family and community. In today's busy world, where schedules are often frantic and families are scattered, the family meal serves as a vital anchor, a

consistent time for connection and shared experience. It's a space where children feel heard, understood, and valued. The shared experience of food, laughter, and conversation strengthens bonds and fosters a sense of belonging.

Beyond the daily rituals, annual traditions hold an even deeper significance. Think of the family vacation, a yearly pilgrimage to a cherished destination, creating a shared history and a collection of precious memories. These traditions become markers of time, milestones in a family's journey together. They provide a sense of continuity, connecting generations and reinforcing the feeling of shared identity. The anticipation leading up to the event, the shared experience of travel, the creation of new memories – all of these contribute to the strengthening of family bonds. These shared experiences create a narrative, a collective story that binds the family together.

Holiday celebrations are another powerful example.

Christmas morning, Hanukkah festivities, Thanksgiving dinner – these are opportunities to engage in meaningful rituals that transcend the everyday. The decorations, the food, the shared activities – they all contribute to a sense of excitement, anticipation, and connection. They are not merely about the celebration itself, but about the shared experience, the collective effort, and the reinforcement of family values. These traditions become anchors, grounding the family in shared beliefs and values.

The creation and maintenance of family rituals is not always effortless. Life's complexities – work schedules, extracurricular activities, unexpected events – can disrupt even the most carefully planned routines. Flexibility is key; rituals should adapt to the ever-changing needs of the family.

The important element is consistency, the commitment to maintaining the connection, even amidst the chaos. The key is to find those rituals that resonate with your family, those traditions that truly reflect your values and aspirations.

Furthermore, it's crucial to involve children in the creation and maintenance of family rituals. Allow them to contribute their ideas, their preferences, their perspectives. This sense of ownership strengthens their connection to the tradition, increasing their investment in its continuation. It's about fostering a sense of collaboration, a shared responsibility for maintaining the fabric of family life. This collaborative approach fosters a sense of belonging and increases their emotional investment in the ritual.

The rituals themselves can be simple or elaborate, depending on the family's preferences and resources. The key is not the complexity of the activity, but the consistency, the intentionality, and the shared experience. A simple weekly game night, a regular nature walk, a shared chore, a nightly story – all of these can contribute to building strong family bonds. It's about finding those moments, those activities that resonate with your family, that foster connection, and that create lasting memories.

Consider the families where these rituals are absent. The lack of structure, the inconsistency, the absence of shared experiences – these can contribute to a sense of isolation, disconnect, and emotional instability. Children in these families may struggle with identity formation, struggle with establishing healthy relationships, and struggle with navigating the complexities of life. They may lack the emotional resilience necessary to overcome challenges, and may find themselves adrift in a sea of uncertainty. The absence of these rituals creates a void, a lack of grounding, a lack of that sense of belonging that is so vital for healthy development.

Then, the establishment and maintenance of family rituals and traditions are not just nice-to-haves; they are essential components of a thriving family unit. They are the mortar that holds the bricks of family life together, creating a strong, supportive, and resilient foundation for children to grow and thrive. They are an investment in the future, an investment in the well-being of each family member, and an investment in the overall health and happiness of the family as a whole. The effort invested in creating meaningful rituals is an investment that will yield immeasurable returns, strengthening bonds, fostering connection, and creating a legacy of love and shared experience that will last a lifetime. The consistent repetition of these rituals creates a deep sense of security and belonging, strengthening family bonds and promoting emotional well-being for each family member.

This shared sense of belonging is crucial for healthy childhood development, helping children build self-esteem and navigate life's challenges with greater resilience.

The creation of these rituals should be a collaborative effort, involving every member of the family. Children should have a voice in choosing the activities and traditions that resonate with them. This shared ownership reinforces the sense of belonging and shared purpose within the family. Involving children in planning and executing the rituals fosters their sense of responsibility and ownership, further strengthening the bonds and creating positive associations with family life. This collaborative approach also teaches valuable life skills such as teamwork, communication, and compromise, further enriching their development.

Moreover, adapting rituals to suit the family's changing needs is crucial for their long-term success. Flexibility allows the rituals to remain relevant and meaningful as the children grow and the family's circumstances evolve. This flexibility ensures that the rituals remain dynamic and adaptable, ensuring they continue to be a source of strength and connection throughout the family's journey. This adaptable approach will prevent the rituals from becoming stale or burdensome, ensuring their continued positive impact on family dynamics.

In essence, the development of strong family rituals and traditions is an ongoing process that requires commitment and intentionality. It is an investment in the emotional well-being of the entire family, creating a strong foundation for lasting connection, shared identity, and a sense of belonging.

By fostering these rituals, families create a powerful and enduring legacy, enriching not only the lives of their children but also their own. The effort expended in creating and maintaining these rituals far outweighs the benefits they provide, shaping the family into a cohesive, supportive unit, capable of weathering life's storms together. The legacy of these rituals, these shared experiences, these moments of connection, will resonate through generations, creating a tapestry of love, belonging, and enduring family bonds.

Beyond Material Wealth

The relentless pursuit of material wealth has become a defining characteristic of our modern era. We're bombarded daily with messages that equate success with financial abundance, a larger house, the latest gadgets, and prestigious titles. This pervasive narrative seeps into our subconscious, subtly shaping our values and influencing our parenting styles. We strive to provide our children with the best things money can buy, often believing that doing so automatically translates to happy, well-adjusted children. But what happens when we prioritize material wealth over genuine emotional connection and nurturing? The answer, sadly, is often a disconnect that leaves a deep, sometimes irreparable, crack in the foundation of our children's lives.

Consider the family perpetually stressed by financial pressures. The parents, working tirelessly to afford a larger house in an upscale neighborhood, might find themselves emotionally unavailable to their children. Dinner conversations are rushed, bedtime stories are replaced by hurried goodnights, and genuine connection is sacrificed at the altar of financial security. The children, sensing the strain and the lack of focused attention, might resort to acting out, seeking attention through disruptive behavior. They crave the emotional nourishment that material possessions simply cannot provide. This isn't to say that financial stability is unimportant; it's crucial for a family's well-being. However, it's a means to an end, not the end itself. When financial security becomes the sole focus, it eclipses the vital role of emotional support, nurturing, and genuine connection.

The irony is that the very things we're striving to achieve – a comfortable lifestyle, a secure future for our children – might inadvertently be undermining the very foundation of their happiness and well-being. A child growing up in a lavish home, yet deprived of genuine emotional connection, might experience a deeper sense of emptiness and insecurity than a child raised in more modest circumstances, but

surrounded by love, support, and strong family bonds. This emotional poverty, this lack of genuine human connection, can be far more damaging than any material hardship.

Think about the child who constantly compares themselves to others, fueled by the constant barrage of curated perfection presented on social media. They see their friends' luxurious vacations, designer clothes, and seemingly effortless achievements, leading to feelings of inadequacy and discontent. This constant comparison game, driven by the relentless pursuit of material success, can lead to anxiety, depression, and a distorted sense of self-worth. The relentless pursuit of "more" can leave a child feeling perpetually dissatisfied, always chasing an elusive ideal of perfection that ultimately remains out of reach.

The pressure to maintain an outward appearance of success, both for the parents and for the children, contributes significantly to this insidious cycle. It's a performance, a carefully constructed facade that masks underlying anxieties and vulnerabilities. Parents might feel pressured to keep up with the Joneses, to provide experiences and possessions that they themselves may not feel comfortable affording,

exacerbating the already existing stress and strain on the family unit. Children, in turn, might feel the pressure to perform, to achieve academically, socially, and athletically, driven not by intrinsic motivation, but by a desperate need to meet the expectations of a performance-driven culture.

Redefining success, then, involves a paradigm shift. It means valuing emotional well-being above material possessions,

prioritizing genuine connections over external validation. It's about fostering resilience, self-esteem, and empathy, and nurturing a child's ability to navigate the complexities of life with confidence and compassion. It's about fostering a sense of belonging within the family unit and building a strong, supportive network of relationships beyond the family.

This involves conscious effort and deliberate choices. It means putting down the phone, turning off the screens, and truly engaging with our children. It means active listening, offering unconditional love and acceptance, and providing the kind of support and guidance that allows them to thrive, not just survive. It means creating opportunities for meaningful interactions, fostering a love of learning, and encouraging them to pursue their passions. It means teaching them the importance of gratitude, empathy, and resilience, helping them to develop a strong sense of self-worth that isn't contingent on external validation.

Creating a home environment that prioritizes emotional well-being involves establishing healthy routines and rituals.

Regular family meals, bedtime stories, shared activities –these small gestures weave the fabric of connection and create lasting memories. It also involves creating a safe space where children feel comfortable expressing their emotions, seeking help when needed, and knowing that they are unconditionally loved and accepted, regardless of their imperfections or challenges.

Mentorship plays a vital role in this process. Children need positive role models who exemplify the values we want them to embody. This could be a parent, a grandparent, a teacher, a coach, or a friend. The influence of these mentors can be profound, shaping a child's character, instilling confidence, and guiding them towards a meaningful life.

It's important to set realistic expectations for our children. Every child is unique, with their own strengths, weaknesses, and developmental trajectory. We must celebrate their achievements, no matter how small, and offer unwavering support during times of difficulty. This approach fosters self-esteem, resilience, and a sense of self-efficacy that will serve them well throughout their lives.

Ultimately, redefining success in the context of parenting involves recognizing the inherent worth of our children, independent of their accomplishments or possessions. It's about acknowledging the profound impact of our actions, both positive and negative, on their emotional well-being and their future happiness. It's about creating a legacy of love, support, and genuine connection, a legacy that will resonate far beyond the accumulation of material wealth. This is the true measure of success – a legacy of emotionally healthy, resilient, and compassionate individuals who are equipped to navigate the complexities of life with grace and understanding. It's a legacy that money simply cannot buy.

Cultivating Emotional Intelligence

The pursuit of material success, as we've discussed, often overshadows the far more crucial aspect of emotional well-being. We've built empires of possessions, yet sometimes find ourselves inhabiting emotional deserts. This is where the cultivation of emotional intelligence becomes paramount, not just for our children, but for ourselves as parents. It's a journey of self-discovery and growth, a process of

understanding and managing our own emotions, and equipping our children with the same vital skills. The ability to recognize, understand, and manage emotions is the cornerstone of a fulfilling life, a life less fractured by the pressures and anxieties of the modern world.

For parents, this starts with self-reflection. Ask yourself: How do I react to stress? Do I lash out in anger, withdraw into silence, or perhaps become overly critical?

Understanding our own emotional responses is the first step towards managing them effectively. Consider journaling your feelings throughout the day, noting triggers and responses. This conscious awareness is crucial; it allows us to identify patterns and develop healthier coping mechanisms. If anger is a recurring issue, perhaps explore anger management techniques like deep breathing exercises or mindfulness meditation. If sadness or anxiety are prevalent, seeking professional guidance from a therapist or counselor could be incredibly beneficial. Remember, we can't teach our children emotional resilience if we haven't cultivated it within ourselves.

This self-awareness then translates to our interactions with our children. Instead of dismissing their emotions as "silly" or "dramatic," we need to validate them. A child's frustration

over a spilled juice, their sadness over a lost toy, or their anger over a perceived injustice – these are all opportunities for teaching. Listen actively, offering empathy and understanding. Reflect their feelings back to them: "You seem really upset that your building blocks fell down. That must be frustrating." This simple act of acknowledging their emotions communicates that their feelings are valid and worthy of attention.

Beyond validation, we need to teach our children the vocabulary of emotions. Help them label their feelings –happy, sad, angry, scared, excited. The more precise their language, the better they can understand and communicate their internal world. Reading books together that explore a wide range of emotions can be incredibly helpful. Discussing characters' feelings in stories allows children to connect with different emotional experiences in a safe and non-threatening environment.

Furthermore, it's crucial to model healthy emotional regulation. When faced with challenging situations, show your children how you navigate your emotions constructively. "Mommy's feeling stressed right now because of work, so I'm going to take a few deep breaths and have a cup of tea to calm down." This transparency allows children to see emotional regulation in action, demonstrating that it's a normal and healthy response to difficult situations. It teaches them that it's okay to feel a wide range of emotions, and that managing those emotions is a skill that can be learned and practiced.

We also need to teach children emotional resilience, the ability to bounce back from adversity. This doesn't mean shielding them from challenges; in fact, it means the opposite. Allowing children to experience setbacks, frustrations, and disappointments, while providing support and guidance, is essential for building resilience. Help them problem-solve, encouraging them to think creatively about how to overcome obstacles. Teach them to view challenges as opportunities for growth, not as insurmountable obstacles. Celebrate their efforts and their perseverance, regardless of the outcome.

Another vital aspect of fostering emotional intelligence is teaching empathy. Encourage children to consider the perspectives of others. Ask questions like, "How do you think your friend feels when you take their toy without asking?" or "What would you do if you were in their shoes?" Role-playing scenarios can be a powerful tool for developing empathy. Engage in community service activities,
volunteering at a local animal shelter or food bank. These experiences expose children to different perspectives and foster a sense of compassion for others.

Screen time, as we've previously discussed, can significantly impact emotional development. Excessive screen time can lead to emotional detachment, reduced empathy, and difficulty regulating emotions. While technology can be a valuable tool, it's crucial to establish healthy boundaries and prioritize face-to-face interactions. Engage in activities that promote emotional connection, such as playing games, reading together, having family dinners, and engaging in shared hobbies. These shared experiences foster strong bonds and create opportunities for emotional growth.

Furthermore, fostering a strong sense of self-esteem is crucial for emotional well-being. Unconditional love and acceptance are the bedrock of healthy self-esteem. Let your children know that you love them regardless of their mistakes or imperfections. Encourage their talents and interests, providing opportunities for them to explore their passions. Help them identify their strengths and build on their successes, fostering a sense of self-efficacy.

Remember that emotional intelligence is not a destination; it's a continuous journey of growth and learning. It's a skill that needs to be nurtured and developed throughout life. As parents, we are the primary role models for our children. By consciously cultivating our own emotional intelligence, we create a supportive and nurturing environment where our children can learn and grow emotionally. This journey
requires patience, understanding, and a commitment to self-reflection. It's a challenging but rewarding process, leading to stronger family relationships and well-adjusted children equipped to navigate the complexities of life with grace, resilience, and empathy. This is the true legacy we should strive to build, a legacy far more valuable than any material possession. It's a legacy of emotional well-being, a legacy that will resonate through generations, building a stronger and more compassionate world, one emotionally intelligent individual at a time. This investment in emotional intelligence is not just about raising successful children; it's about raising happy, healthy, and fulfilled human beings who are capable of contributing meaningfully to the world. It is an investment in a future where empathy, understanding, and emotional resilience are not just ideals, but the cornerstone of a thriving society. And that, my friends, is a success far greater than any material gain. It's a success that truly matters.

The Value of Mentorship

The pursuit of emotional intelligence, as crucial as it is, doesn't exist in a vacuum. It flourishes within a supportive ecosystem, a network of nurturing relationships that guide and inspire a child's growth. This is where the profound value of mentorship comes into play, a concept often overlooked in our fast-paced, achievement-driven society. Mentorship isn't simply about having a successful adult in a child's life; it's about cultivating a deep and meaningful connection built on trust, understanding, and shared
experiences. It's about providing a safe space for growth, a place where vulnerabilities can be shared without judgment, and dreams can be nurtured without cynicism.

Think of a child's life as a delicate sapling. While parental love provides the essential nutrients—the soil and water—mentorship acts as the sunlight and the gentle hand that guides its growth towards the sky. A mentor doesn't replace a parent; instead, they offer a different perspective, a complementary set of skills and experiences. They can be a grandparent, an aunt or uncle, a teacher, a coach, or even a trusted family friend. The key is the quality of the relationship, not necessarily the formal title or connection.

The impact of a positive mentor can be transformative. Consider a child struggling with a particular subject in school. A mentor who excels in that area can provide personalized tutoring, not just in the academic sense, but also in cultivating a positive mindset towards learning. They can instill confidence, break down complex concepts into manageable pieces, and, perhaps most importantly,

demonstrate the value of perseverance. This is far beyond simply achieving good grades; it's about building resilience and a growth mindset—the belief that abilities can be developed through dedication and hard work.

Similarly, a child grappling with social anxieties might find solace and guidance in a mentor who understands and empathizes with their struggles. A mentor can act as a bridge, connecting the child to social circles, teaching valuable social skills, and helping them navigate the complexities of peer relationships. This mentorship might involve casual conversations, shared activities, or even simply providing a safe space for the child to process their emotions and experiences. The mentor's presence can offer a sense of belonging, fostering a feeling of being understood and accepted.

The benefits of mentorship extend far beyond academic or social realms. A mentor can be a source of inspiration, demonstrating the possibilities that lie ahead. They can share their own life experiences, both triumphs and setbacks, offering valuable lessons and insights that a textbook could never impart. This shared journey allows the child to learn from the mentor's successes and mistakes, fostering a deeper understanding of themselves and the world around them. They gain a unique perspective on life's challenges and learn valuable coping mechanisms.

The lack of mentorship can leave a significant void in a child's life, a void that can manifest in various ways. Without a supportive guide, a child might struggle with self-doubt, lack direction, or feel isolated in their struggles. The absence of positive role models can lead to a skewed perception of success, emphasizing material wealth over emotional well-being, mirroring the pitfalls we've already explored. Children without strong mentoring relationships may struggle to develop a strong sense of self-identity, lacking the external validation and guidance needed to navigate their own journey of self-discovery. This can result in feelings of inadequacy, a lack of confidence, and a diminished sense of purpose.

The importance of mentorship is particularly crucial in today's world, where children are bombarded with conflicting messages and pressures. Social media, while offering opportunities for connection, can also contribute to feelings of inadequacy and anxiety. A mentor can provide a counterbalance, offering a realistic perspective on life and providing a safe space away from the often-filtered and unrealistic portrayals of success found online. They can help children develop a healthy relationship with technology, learning to use it responsibly and avoid the potential pitfalls of social comparison and cyberbullying.

Mentorship is not a one-size-fits-all approach. The ideal mentor-mentee relationship is characterized by mutual respect, trust, and a genuine connection. The mentor's role is not to dictate or control, but to guide and empower. They should provide support and encouragement, allowing the child to learn and grow at their own pace. The relationship should be based on shared interests and goals, fostering a sense of camaraderie and mutual respect. It's a collaboration, a partnership in growth, rather than a hierarchical power dynamic.

Finding the right mentor is a journey in itself. It requires a willingness to connect with others, to build relationships, and to seek out individuals who can provide valuable guidance and support. Parents play a crucial role in facilitating this process, encouraging their children to form connections with positive role models and providing opportunities for mentorship to flourish. This might involve arranging opportunities for their children to participate in activities such as sports, arts, or community service, where they can connect with individuals who share their interests and values.

Moreover, parents themselves can actively seek out mentors for their children. This proactive approach demonstrates the importance they place on their child's well-being and development. It's about building a strong network of support for the child, creating a community that nurtures and empowers their growth. This might involve reaching out to teachers, coaches, family friends, or even professionals in fields that align with the child's interests or aspirations.

The cultivation of mentorship is an investment in a child's future, an investment that yields dividends far beyond material success. It's an investment in their emotional well-being, their resilience, their self-confidence, and their ability to navigate the complexities of life with grace and determination. A child with a strong mentoring network is better equipped to overcome challenges, to pursue their dreams with passion, and to contribute meaningfully to the world. This is the true definition of success, a success that resonates far beyond the accumulation of wealth or possessions. It's a legacy of growth, resilience, and

compassion—a legacy that will shape not only the child's life but also the lives of those they touch. This is the essence of creating a truly fulfilling life, a life grounded in emotional intelligence and nurtured by the unwavering support of a strong mentorship network. It is a foundation far stronger and more resilient than any material wealth could ever provide. The absence of this profound support system leaves a significant, often hidden crack in a child's foundation, a crack that can ripple through their entire life trajectory.

Therefore, actively cultivating meaningful mentoring relationships is not just advisable; it's essential.

NINE

SETTING REALISTIC EXPECTATIONS

The shimmering trophy, a testament to young Ethan's chess prowess, sat gleaming on the mantelpiece. It was a beautiful thing, a symbol of triumph, a reflection of countless hours spent hunched over a checkered board, strategizing, calculating, and ultimately, conquering. But the trophy, in its polished perfection, held a hidden truth – a truth that many parents, blinded by the allure of achievement, often overlook. The pursuit of external validation, the relentless striving for excellence measured solely by trophies and accolades, can often overshadow the far more vital aspects of a child's development. Ethan's success was undeniable, but was it truly a measure of his well-being? Was the relentless pressure to win, to always be the best, inadvertently creating a hidden crack in his foundation, a crack that even the brightest trophy couldn't conceal?

This is the crux of redefining success – moving beyond the superficial metrics of achievement and embracing a more holistic view of a child's growth. It's about acknowledging that the journey, with its stumbles and triumphs, is just as important, if not more so, than the destination. It's about nurturing the inner landscape of a child, fostering resilience, empathy, and a genuine love for the process itself, rather than solely focusing on the outcome. Success, in its truest form, is not solely defined by achievements but by the character forged in the crucible of experience, by the lessons learned in both victory and defeat. It is about nurturing a child's inherent abilities, not pushing them to conform to a pre-defined mold of excellence.

Consider the example of Maya, a gifted artist whose parents, driven by their own aspirations of artistic fame, enrolled her in an intense, competitive art program. The pressure was immense. Every brushstroke was scrutinized, every composition dissected, every piece judged against an impossibly high standard. Maya, though talented, began to lose her joy, her creativity stifled by the relentless pressure to perform. Her vibrant, playful style became muted, replaced by a rigid adherence to technical perfection. The fear of failure overshadowed the love of the process, leaving her feeling perpetually inadequate. Her parents, ironically, in their quest for her success, had inadvertently diminished her intrinsic motivation, ultimately undermining her artistic spirit.

True success lies in fostering a love of learning, an intrinsic motivation that propels a child forward, not out of a desire for external validation, but out of a genuine passion for the subject. This intrinsic motivation is a far more powerful engine of growth than any externally imposed pressure. It allows children to develop resilience and to embrace challenges as opportunities for learning and growth, not as threats to their self-worth. When a child fails, as they inevitably will, it should be an opportunity for reflection, for learning from mistakes, and for developing problem-solving skills. This is where the crucial role of parental support comes in.

The support system should be a bedrock of unwavering love and acceptance, providing a safe space for children to experiment, to fail, and to learn without the fear of judgment. This doesn't mean condoning poor behavior; rather, it means responding to setbacks with empathy and guidance, fostering a growth mindset where mistakes are seen as valuable learning experiences. This necessitates a shift in parental perspective, from a focus on achievement to a focus on development. It requires parents to ask themselves: What skills is my child developing? Are they learning to persevere in the face of adversity? Are they becoming more resilient? Are they developing empathy and compassion?

These are far more important indicators of success than any trophy or accolade.

This necessitates a fundamental re-evaluation of our societal norms and expectations. We live in a culture obsessed with achievement, a culture that often values external validation over intrinsic motivation. We celebrate success in terms of material wealth and professional achievements, often neglecting the equally important aspects of emotional well-being, social skills, and personal fulfillment. This cultural bias seeps into our homes, influencing our parenting styles and shaping our expectations of our children. We need to challenge this bias, to recognize that success is far more multifaceted than we often perceive it to be.

Consider the example of Liam, who, unlike his high- achieving peers, chose a less conventional path. He wasn't interested in the Ivy League; instead, he pursued his passion for woodworking, learning the craft from a local artisan. His path was less glamorous, less lucrative, but it was deeply fulfilling. He found joy in the process, in the feel of the wood in his hands, in the transformation of raw materials into beautiful, functional objects. His parents, initially apprehensive, came to recognize the value of his chosen path, seeing the intrinsic motivation and self-reliance it fostered. Liam's success, though not measured in conventional terms, was undeniably profound. He had found his passion, developed valuable skills, and cultivated a deep sense of self-worth.

This is the essence of setting realistic expectations: accepting the unique individuality of each child. Each child possesses a unique set of strengths, weaknesses, and interests. Pushing a child to conform to a pre-defined mold of success not only undermines their individuality but also inhibits their growth.

Instead, parents should nurture their child's unique talents and interests, creating a space for them to explore their passions and develop their skills at their own pace. This means acknowledging that not every child is destined for academic excellence or athletic prowess. Some may flourish in the arts, others in the trades, while still others may find their calling in community service or entrepreneurship.

Setting realistic expectations also means accepting that setbacks are inevitable and that failure is a valuable learning experience. Instead of shielding children from adversity, parents should help them navigate challenges, developing their resilience and problem-solving skills. This involves fostering a growth mindset, where challenges are seen as opportunities for learning and growth, rather than threats to self-worth. It means teaching children to view failure not as a reflection of their inherent abilities but as a stepping stone toward future success. This perspective shift is crucial in helping children develop a sense of self-efficacy, the belief in their own ability to succeed.

Furthermore, realistic expectations mean understanding that children develop at their own pace. Comparing children to their peers, whether siblings or classmates, is detrimental to their self-esteem and can create unnecessary pressure. Every child has a unique developmental trajectory, and parents should celebrate their progress and achievements at their own pace, rather than focusing on comparisons. This involves recognizing individual strengths and weaknesses and tailoring support accordingly. It requires patience, empathy, and a willingness to adapt to each child's unique needs.

Finally, setting realistic expectations involves appreciating the intrinsic rewards of learning and growth. While external rewards, such as trophies or accolades, can be motivating, they should not be the sole focus of a child's efforts. Parents should cultivate a love of learning for its own sake, fostering a sense of curiosity, creativity, and exploration. This means prioritizing activities that are enjoyable and engaging, rather than those that are solely focused on achievement. It's about encouraging children to pursue their interests, to develop their talents, and to discover their passions. This is where the true essence of success lies: not in the pursuit of external validation, but in the intrinsic fulfillment of personal growth and self-discovery. The trophy on the mantelpiece is nice, but the real treasure lies in the journey, in the character forged, in the person the child becomes—not what the world tells them they should be. That's the lasting legacy, the true, unbreakable foundation.

Celebrating Small Victories

The quiet triumph of a perfectly tied shoelace. The focused concentration etched on a child's face as they painstakingly color within the lines. The unprompted sharing of a toy, a small act of generosity born not of obligation but of genuine kindness. These are not the headline-grabbing achievements that fill trophy cases or dominate social media feeds. They are, however, the quiet victories, the incremental steps forward that build the foundation of a child's self-esteem and confidence. They are the bricks and mortar of a secure and resilient personality, far more valuable than any external validation.

Many parents, caught in the whirlwind of societal pressures and the constant pursuit of academic excellence, often overlook these seemingly insignificant moments. We are so focused on the grand spectacle, the "A+" on the report card, the winning goal in the soccer game, that we miss the subtle but profound impact of acknowledging the smaller, everyday accomplishments. These small wins, often dismissed as inconsequential, are the very building blocks of a child's self-belief, shaping their perception of their capabilities and their sense of self-worth.

Consider the child who struggles with reading. The frustration, the tears, the sheer effort required to decode words can be immense. For this child, successfully reading a single page, a single sentence, even a single word, is a monumental achievement. It is a victory hard-earned, a testament to perseverance and resilience. To dismiss this accomplishment as trivial is to undervalue the immense effort and courage it represents. Instead, what if we, as parents, made a conscious effort to celebrate this tiny triumph? A simple hug, a genuine word of praise, a celebratory dance – these small gestures can make all the difference, nurturing the seed of self-belief that will blossom into future successes.

Think of the child who is shy and hesitant, who struggles to initiate interactions with their peers. The act of making eye contact, offering a smile, or even just sitting near another child on the playground – these are often small victories that go unnoticed, yet represent a significant step forward. These small, incremental steps require bravery and self- overcoming. The parent who fails to acknowledge these courageous acts risks undermining the child's growing confidence, and inadvertently discouraging future attempts at social interaction. Conversely, a positive response, a warm acknowledgment of their efforts, can embolden the child to continue taking these vital risks. The reward for the parent is not just a more socially adept child, but a child who learns to embrace challenges and step outside of their comfort zone.

The same principle applies across the spectrum of childhood development. From mastering the art of tying shoelaces (a feat requiring significant fine motor skill development and patience) to finally cleaning their room without constant prompting (a demonstration of growing independence and responsibility), each small victory deserves recognition and celebration. This isn't about indulging in excessive praise or creating an environment of unwarranted accolades. It's about fostering a culture of appreciation, acknowledging the effort and perseverance behind every accomplishment, no matter how small.

This also means adjusting our own perspective. We, as adults, often judge success based on external benchmarks: grades, awards, possessions. We have been conditioned to believe that success is a singular, towering achievement, something to be strived for, something to be earned through intense competition and relentless pursuit. But for a child, success is a journey, a gradual unfolding of capabilities, a cumulative effect of countless small victories. It's a tapestry woven from the threads of perseverance, resilience, and self-belief. To focus solely on the grand finale, to neglect the individual threads, is to misunderstand the very nature of childhood growth.

To celebrate small victories means creating a safe and supportive environment where children feel empowered to try new things, to take risks, to fail and learn from their mistakes. It means offering encouragement and positive reinforcement, not just during the moments of triumph, but also during the struggles and setbacks. It's about recognizing the inherent value in the process, in the journey, in the effort itself, rather than solely focusing on the outcome.

This doesn't require extravagant gestures or lavish rewards. A simple "I'm so proud of how hard you worked on that," or "That was a really kind thing to do," can be profoundly impactful. Sharing a special moment together, reading a favorite book, engaging in a playful activity, can all serve as powerful affirmations of the child's worth. These small acts of connection create a powerful message: "You matter, your efforts matter, and I am here to support you every step of the way."

Furthermore, celebrating small victories necessitates a shift in our own mindset, a reassessment of our expectations. Are we setting realistic goals for our children? Are we placing undue pressure on them to achieve beyond their capabilities? Are we inadvertently creating an environment of anxiety and self-doubt by focusing solely on external achievements? The relentless pursuit of perfection, the constant pressure to excel, can ironically hinder a child's development and create a sense of inadequacy, even when they are achieving at high levels.

A shift towards acknowledging the intrinsic rewards of effort, rather than relying solely on external validation, is crucial. This means focusing on the process of learning, the joy of discovery, and the satisfaction of overcoming challenges. A child who learns to find fulfillment in the effort itself, regardless of the outcome, develops a resilience and inner strength that serves them well throughout life. This intrinsic motivation is a far more valuable asset than any external reward.

Consider a child learning to ride a bike. The falls, the scrapes, the frustration – these are all part of the learning process. But the moment they finally find their balance, the sheer joy of gliding effortlessly down the street, that's the culmination of countless small victories. Each attempt, each near-miss, each stumble, contributes to their ultimate success. To overlook these smaller milestones is to diminish the magnitude of their achievement and to undermine their developing confidence. The celebration should be as much about the journey as it is about the destination.

The same applies to academic pursuits. A child struggling with fractions might find immense satisfaction in finally understanding the concept, even if they don't score perfectly on the test. The effort, the perseverance, the gradual acquisition of knowledge – these are the true measures of success. To focus solely on the test score is to miss the forest for the trees, to undervalue the invaluable lessons learned along the way.

Celebrating small victories also means creating opportunities for children to experience success. This might involve adjusting expectations, breaking down tasks into smaller, more manageable steps, providing appropriate support and guidance, and offering encouragement along the way. It's about fostering a growth mindset, where challenges are viewed as opportunities for learning and growth, rather than threats to self-esteem.

It's about embracing the imperfections and celebrating the progress. No child is perfect, and no journey is without its stumbles. But every step forward, no matter how small, contributes to their overall development and self-esteem. Celebrating these small victories cultivates a sense of self-efficacy, a belief in one's ability to succeed. This belief is a powerful antidote to self-doubt and a key ingredient for resilience in the face of adversity.

In essence, celebrating small victories is not about superficial praise or inflating a child's ego. It is about fostering a deep sense of self-worth, nurturing their resilience, and creating a supportive and encouraging environment where they feel empowered to strive for their goals, regardless of the outcome. It is about recognizing the inherent worth of the child and the incredible journey of their development, celebrating every step, every struggle, every small triumph along the way. It is in these quiet victories, these seemingly insignificant moments, that the true foundation of a child's character is laid—a foundation far stronger and more resilient than any trophy ever could be. And that, ultimately, is the truest measure of success.

Seeking Support and Connection

The previous chapter emphasized the vital role of family rituals and traditions in forging strong bonds and creating a sense of belonging. But even the most carefully crafted family routines can't shield against the inevitable storms of life. Stress, illness, financial hardship, and the challenges of raising children in a rapidly changing world can test even the strongest family units. This is where seeking external

support and connection becomes not just beneficial, but essential. Isolation, that insidious enemy of well-being, can silently erode the very foundation of family strength, leaving parents feeling overwhelmed, depleted, and disconnected from their children.

The myth of the "perfect parent" – the individual who effortlessly manages every aspect of family life while maintaining unwavering composure – must be shattered. It's a fantasy that sets unrealistic expectations and leaves many parents feeling inadequate and ashamed when they inevitably fall short. Acknowledging our limitations and actively seeking support is not a sign of weakness; it's a testament to our commitment to our children's well-being and our own emotional health.

Building a robust support network involves cultivating relationships with individuals and groups who can offer understanding, practical assistance, and emotional sustenance. This network might include family members, friends, other parents, mentors, faith-based communities, or professional support systems. Each of these connections plays a unique and valuable role in providing the emotional buffer and practical help needed to navigate the complexities of parenthood.

Grandparents, aunts, uncles, and cousins can provide invaluable assistance with childcare, offering parents much-needed respite and a chance to recharge. They can also serve as role models, sharing their wisdom and experiences, offering a different perspective on parenting challenges. However, it's crucial to remember that these relationships are not always straightforward. Differing parenting styles and generational gaps can sometimes lead to friction. Open communication and a willingness to compromise are vital to harnessing the benefits of extended family support while navigating potential conflicts constructively.

Friends, particularly those who are also parents, can provide a crucial lifeline. They understand the unique pressures and joys of parenthood, offering empathy, practical advice, and a safe space to vent frustrations. Shared experiences create a bond of understanding that transcends casual acquaintanceship. Connecting with other parents through playgroups, parent-teacher associations, or online forums can create a sense of community and shared purpose, fostering a supportive environment where parents can learn from one another and feel less isolated.

Mentorship, whether formal or informal, can provide invaluable guidance and support. A mentor, be it a trusted family friend, a seasoned parent, or a professional in the field, can offer objective perspectives, helping parents navigate difficult decisions and develop effective coping mechanisms. They can provide encouragement and reaffirm a parent's inherent capabilities, helping to build confidence and resilience.

Faith-based communities often offer a rich tapestry of support, providing spiritual guidance, emotional sustenance, and a sense of community. The shared values and beliefs can create a supportive environment where parents can find comfort, encouragement, and practical assistance during challenging times. The rituals and routines inherent in many faith traditions can also provide a framework for strengthening family bonds and creating a sense of belonging.

When personal support networks prove insufficient, accessing professional help is crucial. Therapists, counselors, and parenting coaches can provide valuable tools and strategies for managing stress, resolving conflicts, and fostering healthy parent-child relationships. They offer a confidential space for parents to explore their challenges without judgment, gaining insight and developing effective coping mechanisms. These professionals are trained to identify potential warning signs and offer interventions to prevent escalation of problems.

However, seeking support isn't merely about addressing crises; it's about proactively building resilience. Regularly engaging with your support network, sharing successes and challenges alike, strengthens those bonds and creates a sense of security. This proactive approach allows for early intervention should difficulties arise, preventing minor issues from escalating into major problems. Remember, seeking help is not a sign of failure; it's a demonstration of strength and a commitment to nurturing your family.

Consider the example of Sarah, a single mother working two jobs to provide for her two young children. She felt constantly overwhelmed, struggling to balance work, household chores, and childcare. Her exhaustion manifested in short tempers and a growing distance from her children.

Initially, she felt ashamed to admit her struggles, fearing judgment. However, with the encouragement of a friend, she reached out to a local community center, where she found a

parenting support group and access to subsidized childcare. The support group provided a safe space for her to share her experiences, realizing she wasn't alone in her struggles. The childcare assistance gave her much-needed respite, allowing her to recharge and reconnect with her children. This simple act of seeking help transformed her life, significantly improving her emotional well-being and strengthening her bond with her children.

Think of another scenario, involving John and Mary, a couple struggling with their teenage son's rebellious behavior. Their attempts to communicate and set boundaries seemed to only escalate the conflict. Frustrated and overwhelmed, they felt their relationship with their son was irrevocably damaged. A family therapist helped them understand the underlying dynamics of their family system and develop effective communication strategies. The therapist guided them through conflict resolution techniques and helped them build a stronger, more empathetic connection with their son. Through professional guidance, they were able to transform a strained family dynamic into one of greater understanding and mutual respect.

These examples highlight the transformative power of seeking support and connection. It's not a sign of weakness, but rather a testament to the strength and resilience needed to navigate the complexities of parenthood. The journey of parenthood is a marathon, not a sprint, and acknowledging the need for support along the way is not only acceptable but also essential for building strong and resilient families.

Building this network takes time and effort, but the rewards—a stronger, more resilient family unit—are immeasurable. It is an ongoing investment in the well-being of both parents and children, creating a secure and loving environment where everyone can thrive. The act of reaching out, of acknowledging vulnerability and seeking assistance, is a powerful act of self-care, benefiting not only the parent but the entire family. It's about building a village around your family, a network of support that strengthens the bonds within and creates a resilient foundation capable of weathering any storm. Remember that it's okay to ask for help – it's a sign of strength, not weakness. Your well-being is intrinsically linked to your family's well-being, and actively seeking support is a critical step in nurturing a thriving, loving family environment. The benefits of a strong support system far outweigh the perceived vulnerability of asking for help. It's an investment in the future, building a stronger, more resilient family capable of navigating life's challenges together.

Consider, too, the often overlooked benefit of seeking support for your own emotional well-being. Parents who prioritize their mental and emotional health are better equipped to provide nurturing and consistent care for their children. Burnout, stress, and anxiety can significantly impair a parent's ability to respond effectively to their children's needs. Taking care of yourself isn't selfish; it's a necessary act of self-preservation that benefits the entire family. By attending to your own well-being, you create a more positive and supportive environment for your children to thrive. Remember, you can't pour from an empty cup. Filling your own cup through self-care and seeking support allows you to be the best parent you can be. And in building your own support network, you simultaneously model healthy coping mechanisms and resilience for your children, teaching them the importance of seeking help when needed and cultivating strong, supportive relationships throughout their lives. This becomes a legacy, a generational pattern of seeking help and strengthening bonds, creating resilient and thriving families for generations to come. This cycle of support, this intergenerational understanding, is ultimately the most profound gift you can give to your children – and yourselves.

Recognizing When to Seek Help

Recognizing the complexities of modern life, with its relentless demands and ever-present distractions, it's easy to overlook subtle shifts in our children's behavior. We're juggling careers, finances, and the constant hum of technology, often leaving us feeling overwhelmed and unsure if what we're seeing is a typical phase or something more significant. This chapter is dedicated to helping you navigate that uncertainty, providing a roadmap to recognize when professional help might be beneficial. It's not a sign of failure to seek assistance; it's a testament to your commitment to your child's well-being.

Let's start with the everyday anxieties that frequently plague parents. A child struggling with schoolwork, exhibiting sudden outbursts of anger, or withdrawing socially are common concerns. These behaviors, while sometimes temporary responses to stress or developmental changes, can also indicate deeper underlying issues. Persistent difficulties in focusing, significant changes in appetite or sleep patterns, and unexplained physical complaints might warrant a closer look. The key is to differentiate between normal childhood fluctuations and persistent patterns that disrupt daily life or cause significant distress.

Consider the context. A child's reaction to a specific event, such as a family move or a loss, might manifest as temporary behavioral changes. However, if these behaviors persist long after the event has passed, or if they are extreme and significantly impacting the child's ability to function, seeking professional guidance is often wise. For example, a child who experiences intense anxiety for months after a minor accident may benefit from professional support to help them process their fear and develop coping mechanisms. Similarly, if a teenager exhibits persistent depression or self-harming behaviors following a breakup, professional intervention is crucial.

Think about the intensity and frequency of the behaviors.

Occasional tantrums are a normal part of childhood, but daily, uncontrolled outbursts might point towards an underlying problem. Similarly, occasional bouts of sadness are expected, but prolonged periods of low mood, loss of interest in activities, and feelings of hopelessness could signify depression. The frequency and severity of these behaviors are critical indicators that warrant attention.

Remember that each child is unique, and there is no one-size-fits-all approach to identifying when help is needed.

What constitutes a concerning behavior in one child might be considered normal for another. The most important aspect is paying attention to your child's overall well-being and recognizing changes in their behavior, emotional state, or physical health that cause you significant concern. Trust your parental instincts; if something feels "off," it likely warrants further investigation.

Let's explore some specific examples. Imagine a previously outgoing child suddenly becoming withdrawn and isolating themselves from friends and family. This significant shift in social behavior could indicate depression, social anxiety, or other underlying challenges. Perhaps your child, once a dedicated student, is now consistently underperforming in school despite your efforts. This could suggest learning disabilities, underlying anxiety impacting their ability to focus, or the presence of bullying or other stressful factors. Another scenario might involve a child exhibiting sudden aggression or increased irritability towards family members and peers. While occasional anger is expected, a persistent increase in aggressive behaviors should trigger a discussion with a professional.

The impact on family dynamics also provides a crucial lens through which to assess the need for professional help. If a child's challenging behaviors are straining family relationships, creating conflict, and impacting the well-being of other family members, seeking professional support becomes imperative. The family unit's overall health and functionality should also be a consideration. Persistent arguments, increased tension, or a general sense of unhappiness within the family might signify the need for family therapy. Remember, the well-being of the entire family is interconnected, and addressing a child's challenges often requires a holistic approach.

Beyond specific behaviors, consider your own limitations and resources. If you are feeling overwhelmed, struggling to cope with your child's behavior, or find yourself consistently at your wit's end, it is perfectly acceptable – and even recommended – to seek external support. Parenting is inherently challenging, and acknowledging your limitations is not a sign of weakness but rather a sign of strength.

Remember, seeking professional help is an act of proactive care, demonstrating your dedication to providing your child with the best possible support. Don't hesitate to reach out for assistance when you need it.

The stigma surrounding mental health continues to be a significant barrier for many families. The notion that seeking help equates to failure is a deeply entrenched myth. In reality, seeking professional help shows strength, responsibility, and a commitment to your child's well-being.

It's crucial to remember that mental health challenges are common, and seeking assistance is a proactive step toward resolving them. The earlier you address these challenges, the better the chances of positive outcomes.

Furthermore, remember that professional support isn't just for children with significant issues. Even if your child is generally well-adjusted, accessing support during challenging periods, such as the transition to a new school, a significant life event, or a period of heightened stress, can prove invaluable. Seeking professional guidance provides access to objective perspectives, specialized tools, and strategies to navigate these situations effectively.

Finally, consider the impact of your own mental health.

Parents who are experiencing burnout, stress, or mental health challenges themselves may find it more difficult to provide consistent and nurturing care for their children. Prioritizing your own well-being is not selfish; it's essential for effective parenting. Seeking support for your own mental health can indirectly benefit your child. It creates a more supportive and stable environment for your family and allows you to approach parenting with renewed energy and perspective. Remember that taking care of yourself is an essential component of effective parenting and fosters a healthy family dynamic. Don't hesitate to seek help for yourself, so you can be the best parent you can be.

TEN

FINDING THE RIGHT RESOURCES

The decision to seek professional help is a significant step, a testament to your commitment to your child's well-being. But knowing whereto find the right support can feel overwhelming. The landscape of mental health services is vast and varied, and navigating it can be confusing, particularly when you're already grappling with the anxieties that prompted you to seek help in the first place. This section is designed to empower you with the knowledge and tools to find qualified, compassionate professionals who can provide the support your family needs.

First, consider the specific needs of your child. Are you concerned about behavioral issues, anxiety, depression, learning difficulties, or something else entirely? Identifying the core issue will help you narrow your search. For example, if your child is struggling academically, you might seek out an educational psychologist specializing in learning disabilities. If behavioral problems are the primary concern, a child therapist or behavioral specialist could be the most appropriate choice. Don't hesitate to reach out to your pediatrician or family doctor. They often have a network of professionals they can recommend based on their experience and knowledge of local resources. They can offer valuable insights and referrals, potentially saving you significant time and energy in your search.

Your pediatrician or family doctor might suggest a range of professionals, and understanding the nuances between them is crucial. A child psychologist typically holds a doctoral degree in psychology and is trained to assess and treat

mental health issues in children. They often utilize evidence-based therapies like play therapy, depending on the child's age and needs.

A child therapist, on the other hand, might hold a master's degree in social work or counseling and employs various therapeutic approaches. The specific approach used will vary greatly depending on the therapist's training and the child's unique circumstances.

In addition to psychologists and therapists, consider the role of other professionals. If your child is struggling academically, an educational psychologist can assess their learning styles and identify any underlying learning disabilities. They can then collaborate with the school to develop an individualized education program that caters to the child's specific needs. Occupational therapists can assist with improving fine motor skills, sensory processing, and overall daily living skills, often beneficial for children with developmental delays or sensory sensitivities. Speech-language pathologists focus on

communication disorders, helping children improve their speech, language, and communication skills.

The next crucial step is conducting thorough research. Once you have a clearer understanding of the type of professional you need, it's time to start searching. Your insurance provider's website is an excellent starting point. Many insurance plans offer directories of in-network providers, allowing you to filter by specialty, location, and other criteria. Online directories such as Psychology Today or Zocdoc also provide extensive listings of therapists and counselors, often including profiles, client reviews, and specialties. When reviewing these profiles, pay close attention to the therapist's experience working with children and adolescents, their therapeutic approach, and their expertise in addressing the specific issues your child is facing. Don't hesitate to read client reviews and testimonials, but remember that each child and family are unique, and a therapist's effectiveness can vary from person to person.

Beyond online resources, consider tapping into your personal network. Talk to friends, family members, and other parents. Word-of-mouth recommendations can be invaluable, offering personal insights and firsthand experiences that can be more impactful than online reviews. Your child's school counselor or school psychologist can also be a valuable resource. They are often familiar with local therapists and counselors who have successfully worked with students facing similar challenges. They can offer personalized recommendations tailored to your child's specific needs and the school environment.

Once you've compiled a list of potential professionals, it's time to reach out and schedule initial consultations. Most therapists offer a brief consultation, often at a reduced fee or even free of charge, to discuss your concerns and determine if they're a good fit for your family. During this initial
consultation, consider the following: Do you feel comfortable talking to this person? Do they actively listen to your concerns? Do they clearly explain their approach to therapy? Do they seem to genuinely understand your child's needs? Trust your gut feeling. The therapeutic relationship is crucial to the success of therapy, and choosing a professional you feel comfortable with is essential.

Don't be afraid to ask questions. Inquire about their experience working with children of similar ages, their therapeutic approach, their fees, and their cancellation policy. It's perfectly acceptable, even encouraged, to interview several professionals before making a decision.

Finding the right therapist is a process, and finding the perfect fit shouldn't be rushed.

The financial aspect of seeking professional help is a significant consideration for many families. Explore all possible avenues for financial assistance. Many therapists offer sliding-scale fees based on income, making their services more accessible to families with limited financial resources. Check with your insurance provider to understand your coverage, and inquire about co-pays, deductibles, and out-of-pocket expenses. Some community health centers or non-profit organizations offer reduced-fee or free mental health services to those who qualify. Don't let financial concerns prevent you from seeking the help your child needs. There are resources available to help you navigate these challenges.

Remember, seeking professional help is a sign of strength, not weakness. It demonstrates your commitment to your child's well-being and your willingness to take proactive steps to address challenges. Finding the right resources may require some time and effort, but the rewards—a healthier, happier child, and a stronger, more resilient family—are immeasurable. The journey towards a brighter future for your child begins with taking this vital first step. Don't underestimate the power of seeking support, and remember that you're not alone in this. Many parents face similar challenges, and a wealth of support exists to guide you through this process. Embrace the opportunity to learn and grow, and remember that you are your child's greatest advocate. Finding the right resources is the key to unlocking a path towards healing, growth, and a more fulfilling family life.

The process of seeking professional help is often a journey of discovery, a process of trial and error in finding the best fit for your family's unique needs. Don't be discouraged if the first therapist you try isn't the right match. It's perfectly acceptable to switch therapists if you feel the relationship isn't working, or if your child isn't responding well to the chosen therapeutic approach. Remember, the goal is to find a professional who creates a safe, supportive environment where your child feels comfortable opening up and engaging in the therapeutic process. This process requires patience, understanding and self-compassion. Give yourselves time, explore various options, and trust your instincts. The
investment in your child's well-being is an investment in the future of your entire family.

Furthermore, consider the impact of the therapist's personality on your child. A warm, empathetic, and engaging therapist can create a more welcoming and encouraging atmosphere, facilitating the therapeutic process. While qualifications are undoubtedly important, the personal connection between therapist and child is equally crucial.

Look for someone who connects with your child on a personal level, creating a strong therapeutic alliance.

Finally, maintain open communication with the therapist throughout the treatment process. Regular check-ins and updates allow you to track your child's progress and make adjustments as needed. Don't hesitate to voice your concerns or ask questions. The therapist is a partner in your child's journey towards well-being, and a strong collaborative relationship between you and the therapist is key to successful outcomes. This collaborative approach ensures that all parties are working together towards a common goal—supporting the child's growth and development.

Remember, the journey to better mental well-being is a collaborative one, involving parents, therapists, and of course, the child. Keep the lines of communication open, and remember that it's a journey, not a race. Celebrate small victories, and remain patient and understanding throughout the process.

Navigating the Therapeutic Process

The initial sessions often feel like an exploratory journey. Think of it as mapping uncharted territory. The therapist will want to understand your child's history, their current struggles, and the impact these challenges have on your family. Be prepared to share details, even those that feel uncomfortable or insignificant. Every piece of the puzzle contributes to a clearer picture. Remember that judgment is not part of the equation; the therapist's role is to listen, understand, and help you navigate this complex landscape.

Don't be surprised if the therapist asks seemingly unrelated questions. They may inquire about your child's sleep patterns, appetite, friendships, school performance, and even your family dynamics. This holistic approach acknowledges that mental health isn't isolated; it's interwoven with every aspect of a child's life. A seemingly minor detail – a sudden aversion to a favorite food, a change in sleep habits, or a withdrawn behavior – can offer crucial insights into the underlying issues. Be patient and open, allowing the therapist to build a complete understanding. This comprehensive assessment lays the foundation for an effective treatment plan.

The therapist may also want to involve your child directly in the process, tailoring the approach based on their age and developmental stage. Younger children may benefit from play therapy, a technique that utilizes games and creative activities to help them express their emotions and experiences. Older children and adolescents may engage in more traditional talk therapy, exploring their thoughts and feelings through conversation. The key is finding a method that resonates with your child, making them feel comfortable

and safe enough to open up. Remember, building rapport and trust is paramount to the success of any therapeutic intervention.

Once the therapist has a comprehensive understanding of your child's situation, they will develop a personalized treatment plan. This plan is not a rigid prescription; rather, it's a dynamic roadmap that can be adjusted as needed. It might incorporate various techniques, depending on your child's needs and the underlying issues. Cognitive Behavioral Therapy, for example, helps children identify and challenge negative thought patterns, replacing them with more positive and realistic ones. Play therapy, as mentioned, can be particularly effective for younger children. Family therapy, involving the entire family, may be beneficial in addressing systemic issues within the family dynamic. The therapist will explain each aspect of the treatment plan clearly, ensuring you understand the goals and strategies involved. Ask questions; don't hesitate to express any concerns you may have. The more actively involved you are, the more effective the treatment will be.

The therapeutic process isn't always linear; expect ups and downs. There will be days when your child seems to be making progress, demonstrating positive changes in behavior and mood. And there will be days when setbacks occur; frustration may set in, and old patterns may resurface. This is a normal part of the journey, a testament to the complexity of human emotions and behavior. Remember that progress isn't always measured in dramatic leaps and bounds; sometimes, it's about subtle shifts, small victories that accumulate over time. Celebrate these small wins, reinforcing your child's progress and your family's shared commitment to healing.

Maintaining open communication with your child is crucial throughout the process. Encourage them to express their feelings and experiences, offering a safe and supportive space for them to share their thoughts without judgment.

Listen attentively, validating their emotions, even if you don't necessarily understand or agree with them. Sometimes, simply being present, offering a listening ear and unwavering support, can make a profound difference.

Remember, your child is not alone in this journey; you're a vital part of their support system, offering strength, encouragement, and unwavering love.

Your role extends beyond just listening; actively participate in the therapy process. Attend family therapy sessions, if applicable, contributing your insights and perspectives. Work with the therapist to implement strategies learned

during sessions, creating a consistent approach at home. This
consistent approach ensures that the messages and strategies your child receives in therapy are reinforced at home, creating a cohesive and supportive environment.

Inconsistency can undermine progress, creating confusion and frustration for your child. Therefore, active parental participation is essential for optimal results.

Remember the importance of self-care during this process.

Parenting a child struggling with emotional or behavioral challenges can be emotionally draining. Prioritize your own well-being; find healthy outlets for stress, whether it's exercise, meditation, spending time in nature, or connecting with supportive friends or family members. Neglecting your own well-being can negatively impact your ability to support your child effectively. A strong, healthy parent is better equipped to navigate the challenges of supporting a child through therapeutic intervention. Remember, you are not alone in this journey; seeking support for yourself is a sign of strength, not weakness.

The length of therapy varies considerably, depending on the complexity of the issues, the child's response to treatment, and various other factors. There's no magic timeframe; some children may require a few sessions, while others may benefit from longer-term support. Be patient and trust the process. Regular check-ins with the therapist allow you to monitor your child's progress and make necessary
adjustments along the way. Don't hesitate to express your concerns or ask questions; open communication with the therapist is crucial for a successful outcome. Remember, the therapist is a partner in your child's journey, and a collaborative relationship between you and the therapist is key to successful outcomes.

Throughout this process, remember to celebrate the small victories. Acknowledge and appreciate the positive changes, no matter how small they may seem. A slight improvement in mood, a more positive interaction with a sibling, or a newfound willingness to engage in activities – these are all signs of progress, indicators that the therapeutic intervention is having a positive impact. Celebrate these milestones, reinforcing the positive changes and providing your child with the encouragement they need to continue their journey.

The therapeutic process is a journey, not a race. There will be moments of frustration, setbacks, and challenges. But remember that with patience, consistency, and a collaborative effort, you can guide your child towards a healthier, happier future. Maintain open communication, celebrate the small wins, and never underestimate the power of your love and support. The journey may be challenging, but the destination – a stronger, more resilient child – is worth the effort. The therapeutic process offers not only healing for your child but also a valuable opportunity for growth and learning for the entire family. Embrace the journey, and remember that you are not alone. The support network of professionals and your unwavering love will provide the strength and guidance needed to navigate this path together. The commitment to this journey demonstrates your profound love and dedication to your child's well-being, a testament to the unbreakable bond that unites you. This process is an investment in your child's future, a commitment to their long-term happiness and well-being, and a powerful affirmation of your love and dedication as a parent. Trust in the process, believe in your child's resilience, and remember that you are capable of guiding them through this chapter of their life.

Support Groups and Communities

The therapist's words echoed in my mind: "You're not alone." It was a simple phrase, yet it held the weight of a revelation. Until that point, the struggles of parenting – the anxieties, the self-doubt, the sheer exhaustion – had felt like a solitary burden. I'd envisioned navigating this turbulent sea alone, battling the waves of my child's challenges without a lifeline. But the therapist's gentle reassurance opened a door to a different perspective, one where I could find solace and strength in the shared experiences of other parents.

This realization led me to the discovery of a world I hadn't known existed – a network of support groups and online communities specifically designed for parents facing similar challenges. It was a breathtaking shift from the isolating experience I had been enduring. Suddenly, the silent battles I'd been fighting became conversations, the overwhelming feelings of inadequacy transformed into shared vulnerabilities, and the sense of loneliness melted away in a wave of collective understanding.

My first experience with a support group was somewhat hesitant. I walked into the room, a mix of trepidation and hope churning within me. The air was thick with a quiet energy, a shared unspoken understanding that transcended the initial awkwardness of introductions. The facilitator, a warm and empathetic woman with years of experience supporting families, gently guided us through a structured session. We began with introductions, each person briefly sharing their reason for being there. The stories were varied, unique, yet woven together by a common thread of parental worry and the yearning for connection.

One mother spoke about her teenage daughter's struggles with anxiety. Another shared her frustrations with her son's defiant behavior. A third confessed to feeling overwhelmed by the demands of juggling work and family life. Hearing their stories, I felt a profound sense of relief. I wasn't alone in my struggles; others were facing similar battles, wrestling with similar doubts, and experiencing similar triumphs and defeats. The weight on my shoulders seemed to lessen with each shared confession.

The sessions themselves offered a safe space to vent frustrations, share experiences, and receive practical advice. We discussed coping mechanisms, strategies for dealing with specific behaviors, and resources that could provide additional support. More than just practical advice, however, the group provided an emotional lifeline. The simple act of being heard, understood, and validated proved incredibly therapeutic. Knowing that others understood my struggles, that they had experienced similar difficulties and had found ways to navigate them, gave me hope and renewed my determination.

The group also fostered a sense of community. We shared laughter, tears, and a collective journey through the complexities of parenthood. Bonds formed between strangers united by the shared experience of raising children in today's world. We discovered that the challenges we faced were not unique; they were common experiences that many parents encountered. This realization shifted my perspective from one of isolation to one of collective resilience.

Beyond in-person groups, the digital landscape opened up a whole new world of support. Online forums, social media groups, and parenting websites provided a 24/7 source of connection and information. These spaces offered anonymity for those who felt uncomfortable sharing in a face-to-face setting, making them accessible to a wider range of parents. The anonymity also allowed for a more candid and honest sharing of experiences, without the fear of judgment.

I found myself spending hours scrolling through threads, reading posts from parents grappling with similar issues. Sometimes, I simply read and absorbed their stories, finding comfort in the knowledge that I wasn't alone. Other times, I actively participated, sharing my own experiences and offering support to others. The exchange of information, advice, and emotional support was invaluable. Online communities became a source of information, a space for connecting with experts and peers, and an environment for cultivating a sense of belonging.

One particularly helpful online community focused on mindful parenting. The members shared articles, books, and techniques for managing stress, improving communication, and fostering connection with their children. We exchanged tips on creating a calm and nurturing home environment, techniques for managing conflict, and strategies for promoting emotional intelligence in our children.

The online forum provided an ongoing source of inspiration and support. I learned new strategies for managing my own stress, improving my communication skills, and fostering a stronger connection with my child. The community became an invaluable source of learning and self-improvement, not just for my child, but for myself as well.

I participated in discussions about the challenges of balancing screen time, the difficulties of setting boundaries, and the importance of creating a supportive and loving family environment. These conversations provided a constant reminder that the journey of parenting is a shared experience, a collective effort to raise resilient, capable, and compassionate children.

The support groups and online communities weren't merely a source of advice and strategies; they were a powerful antidote to the isolation and self-doubt that had previously weighed me down. The shared experiences and mutual support helped me see my struggles in a new light, transforming challenges into opportunities for growth and learning. The knowledge that I wasn't alone in my struggles, that others had navigated similar paths and had found a way through, provided immeasurable comfort and inspiration.

The sense of community fostered by these groups was profoundly enriching. It wasn't just about receiving advice; it was about connecting with people who understood my struggles and validated my experiences. The friendships formed within these communities provided a valuable source of ongoing support and encouragement.

I learned that seeking professional help was not a sign of failure but a sign of strength and commitment to my child's well-being. I also discovered the power of community, the strength found in shared experiences, and the healing power of mutual support. The journey wasn't easy, but knowing I wasn't alone, that I had a network of support to rely on, made all the difference.

The insights gained from professional guidance, coupled with the emotional support and practical advice offered within support groups and online communities, helped me transform my approach to parenting. I learned the importance of self-care, setting realistic expectations, and celebrating the small victories along the way.

The journey of parenthood is never straightforward, filled with unexpected twists and turns. But armed with professional guidance and a supportive community, I am confident in my ability to navigate the challenges and nurture my child's growth into a healthy and happy adult. The "hidden crack" in our family's foundation, once a source of anxiety and despair, is gradually healing. The combined strength of professional help and the power of collective support is creating a stronger, more resilient family, united in love and mutual understanding. The journey continues, but the path is now clearer, illuminated by the light of shared experiences and the warm glow of community support.

The support I received extended beyond the immediate realm of my child's challenges. It helped me become a more self-aware, emotionally intelligent parent, equipped to handle the inevitable stresses and complexities of family life.

I learned to prioritize self-care, recognizing that my own well-being was intrinsically linked to my ability to nurture my child.

This journey also taught me the importance of communication, not only with my child but also with my partner and other family members. Open dialogue became a cornerstone of our family dynamic, fostering understanding and mutual support. Learning to express my needs and anxieties, both within the supportive community and within my own family, proved to be a vital step in creating a stronger, more resilient family unit.

In conclusion, the path to effective parenting involves a multifaceted approach. It's not solely about finding the right strategies or techniques; it's about fostering a supportive network, nurturing your own well-being, and embracing the power of collective support. The combination of professional guidance, the strength gained from shared experiences in support groups, and the ongoing connection found in online communities created a powerful force that transformed our family's journey. It's a journey that continues, but it's now one navigated with confidence, compassion, and the unwavering support of a community that understands and empathizes with the ups and downs of modern parenting. The "hidden crack" is mending, one shared experience, one supportive conversation, one moment of collective understanding at a time.

Self-Care for Parents

The journey toward healthier parenting, as I've come to understand, isn't just about fixing our children; it's about mending ourselves. The therapist's emphasis on seeking professional help was only half the battle. The other, equally crucial, half resides in the often-neglected realm of self-care.

For months, I'd been so focused on navigating my child's difficulties that I'd completely forgotten to tend to my own emotional and physical well-being. I was running on empty, a depleted reservoir trying to pour out love and support, with nothing left to replenish myself. The result was a vicious cycle: the more drained I became, the less effective I was as a parent.

This realization hit me like a ton of bricks. It wasn't enough to seek external help; I needed to actively cultivate self-care practices into my daily routine. It wasn't about indulgence; it was about survival. It was about recognizing that I couldn't pour from an empty cup. The image of a flight attendant instructing passengers to secure their own oxygen masks before assisting others suddenly became crystal clear in the context of parenting.

The initial steps felt awkward, almost alien. I started small, with seemingly insignificant acts of self-compassion. A long, hot bath became a ritual, a sanctuary where the day's anxieties could melt away with the steam. I rediscovered the joy of reading, losing myself in the pages of a book instead of scrolling endlessly through social media, a constant source of comparison and judgment. Even the simple act of drinking a cup of tea in quiet contemplation became a powerful moment of self-nurturing.

These seemingly insignificant acts accumulated, building a foundation of self-awareness and self-compassion. I started to notice the subtle cues my body sent – the tension in my shoulders, the tightness in my chest, the relentless fatigue that had become my constant companion. These were not just physical sensations; they were signals from my overworked mind and body, pleading for attention and care.

I began to incorporate regular exercise into my routine, not with the goal of achieving a certain physique, but as a means of releasing pent-up stress and anxiety. A brisk walk in nature, a yoga session, or even a simple dance-along to my favorite music became my escape valves, releasing the pressure cooker of daily parenting demands. The physical exertion cleared my head, providing mental space and a renewed sense of energy.

Sleep became another battleground. For months, I had been sacrificing sleep, prioritizing the needs of my child over my own. But sleep deprivation exacerbates stress, diminishes patience, and impairs judgment. I started prioritizing sleep, even if it meant sacrificing some other aspects of my routine. I established a consistent bedtime routine, creating a calming environment conducive to restful sleep. The impact was profound. With sufficient sleep, I felt more capable, more patient, and more present as a parent.

Nutrition also became a priority. I had been neglecting my dietary needs, relying on convenience foods and skipping meals. This, I discovered, significantly impacted my energy levels and mood. I began making conscious choices to nourish my body with healthy, wholesome foods. Cooking became a mindful act, a way to connect with myself and my family through the preparation and sharing of nourishing meals.

Beyond these physical aspects of self-care, I recognized the importance of emotional and mental well-being. I explored mindfulness practices, learning to be present in the moment and to observe my thoughts and feelings without judgment. Meditation, initially a daunting prospect, gradually became a source of calm and clarity. It allowed me to detach from the whirlwind of daily anxieties, creating space for self-reflection and emotional regulation.

I also reconnected with my passions and interests, activities that had been relegated to the sidelines in the relentless demands of parenting. I rediscovered my love for painting, spending quiet evenings lost in the creative process. This provided a much-needed outlet for emotional expression and a sense of accomplishment outside the realm of parenting.

These activities weren't mere distractions; they were vital sources of self-renewal and a reminder of my identity beyond the role of a parent.

Seeking out social support became another crucial aspect of my self-care journey. I joined a local parent support group, initially hesitant but quickly discovering the power of shared experiences. It was incredibly liberating to share my struggles and hear the echoes of my own experiences in the stories of other parents. The sense of community and understanding was invaluable, a lifeline in the sometimes-isolating world of parenting. We shared tips, offered encouragement, and simply listened to each other, creating a supportive network that helped alleviate the weight of our shared burdens.

The journey of self-care wasn't a linear one. There were days when I slipped back into old habits, days when exhaustion and overwhelm took over. But the crucial difference was that now, I recognized these slip-ups as temporary setbacks, not failures. I learned to be kind to myself, to forgive myself, and to gently guide myself back to the path of self-compassion. I understood that self-care wasn't a luxury; it was a necessity. It wasn't selfish; it was an act of self-preservation.

Learning to prioritize self-care wasn't just about improving my own well-being; it had a profound impact on my relationship with my child. With renewed energy and emotional resilience, I was better equipped to handle the challenges of parenting. I was more patient, more present, and more capable of offering the unconditional love and support my child needed. The "hidden crack" I'd feared was slowly mending, not just through professional help and support groups, but also through the simple, yet profoundly powerful, act of taking care of myself.

This process of self-discovery was, and continues to be, a journey of continuous learning. I've come to understand that self-care isn't a destination; it's a lifelong practice, a commitment to nurturing my own well-being, so I can better nurture the well-being of my child and my family. It's about finding the balance between giving and receiving, between selflessness and self-preservation. It's about recognizing that the most precious gift I can offer my child is a parent who is emotionally healthy, resilient, and capable of offering unconditional love. It's about acknowledging that a strong foundation for a child begins with a strong foundation for the parent. It's a journey I'm still on, a journey that evolves and adapts as my child grows, a journey that reminds me that the most powerful act of love I can perform is to take care of myself. And that, I've discovered, is a gift that keeps on giving, not only to me but to my entire family. The echoes of this understanding resonate within our home, creating a harmonious environment where self-care becomes a shared practice, a testament to the transformative power of nurturing oneself in order to better nurture others. It's a testament to the idea that a parent's well-being is intrinsically linked to the well-being of their child, a symbiotic relationship that underscores the importance of prioritizing self-care, not as an indulgence but as a fundamental element of responsible and effective parenting. This realization changed everything.

Building a Strong Foundation

The seeds of a fulfilling and successful adult life are sown not in the abundance of material possessions, but in the fertile ground of a strong emotional and social foundation. This foundation, painstakingly built during childhood, acts as a bedrock upon which a child constructs their self-esteem, resilience, and ability to form meaningful relationships. It's a cornerstone that influences everything from academic
achievement and career success to their capacity for love, empathy, and navigating life's inevitable challenges.

Neglecting this foundation, even subtly, creates that 'hidden crack' – a fissure that, left unaddressed, can widen into a chasm, jeopardizing a child's future.

This isn't about creating a pressure cooker environment, forcing children into a mold of perfection. It's about providing a nurturing environment where a child feels safe to explore, to stumble, and to learn from their mistakes. It's about fostering a deep and genuine connection, characterized by active listening, empathy, and unwavering support, even during moments of frustration or conflict. It's a process that demands mindful attention, consistent effort, and a willingness to adapt to the unique needs and personality of each child.

Think of a sturdy house; strong walls, a solid foundation, a reliable roof. Each component works in harmony, ensuring stability and protection. Similarly, a child's development thrives when emotional security, healthy boundaries, and consistent guidance are woven together. Emotional security forms the foundation – the unwavering feeling of being loved, accepted, and valued, irrespective of their
achievements or mistakes. This sense of security allows
them to take risks, experiment, and grow without fear of judgment or rejection. Healthy boundaries act as the walls, providing structure, guidance, and protection against potential harm. These boundaries aren't about control; they are about teaching self-discipline, responsibility, and respect for others. Consistent guidance acts as the roof, providing shelter from life's storms and directing their growth. This guidance isn't about dictating every decision; it's about providing a compass, helping them navigate life's complexities and make informed choices.

The absence of even one of these crucial elements can weaken the entire structure. A child lacking emotional security might become anxious, withdrawn, or exhibit disruptive behaviors as a cry for attention and validation. A child without healthy boundaries might struggle with self-control, impulsive decisions, and difficulty in forming healthy relationships. A child without consistent guidance might feel lost, directionless, and susceptible to negative influences.

Consider the stark contrast between two scenarios. In the first, a child grows up in a household where parents consistently prioritize quality time, engage in meaningful conversations, and offer unconditional love. They establish clear and consistent boundaries, providing both support and guidance. This child learns self-regulation, develops strong emotional intelligence, and builds confidence in their abilities. They're equipped to navigate challenges, form healthy relationships, and achieve their goals.

In the second scenario, a child grows up in a household where parents are perpetually preoccupied with work, relying on technology to fill the void in their relationship. Boundaries are inconsistent or nonexistent, resulting in

a lack of discipline and emotional instability. This child struggles with self-esteem, lacks the necessary tools to cope with stress, and may display behavioral problems or
difficulties forming meaningful connections. Their path to adulthood is fraught with challenges, making it difficult to navigate relationships, manage their emotions, or achieve their full potential.

The long-term impact of a strong foundation extends far beyond childhood. Children with a secure attachment to their parents, developed through consistent affection, responsive care, and secure boundaries, are more likely to develop strong self-esteem and a positive self-image. This translates into greater resilience in the face of adversity, enabling them to bounce back from setbacks and pursue their goals with determination.

Furthermore, a strong foundation in childhood significantly contributes to successful relationships. Children who have experienced unconditional love and consistent support are better equipped to form healthy, mutually respectful relationships in their adult lives. They understand the importance of communication, empathy, and compromise, characteristics crucial for navigating the complexities of romantic relationships, friendships, and family dynamics.

Academically, a strong foundation is equally significant.

Children who feel secure and supported in their family environments are typically more motivated, focused, and resilient in their studies. They are more likely to approach challenges with a growth mindset, embracing setbacks as opportunities for learning and growth. This positive attitude towards learning extends far beyond the classroom, contributing to their overall success in their chosen career paths.

The ripple effect of a strong foundation extends even into their roles as parents. Individuals raised in nurturing environments are more likely to adopt healthy parenting styles, breaking the cycle of unhealthy patterns that might have been present in their own upbringing. They are better equipped to provide their own children with the emotional support, guidance, and secure attachment that fostered their own well-being.

In essence, building a strong foundation during childhood is an investment in a child's entire future. It's about equipping them with the tools they need to thrive in all aspects of their lives, to navigate challenges with resilience, and to build fulfilling and meaningful relationships. While the journey of parenting is fraught with complexities and challenges, the reward of witnessing a child flourish into a confident,
capable, and compassionate adult is immeasurable. The effort invested in building this foundation is not just a parental responsibility; it's a gift that keeps on giving, enriching not only the child's life, but the lives of those around them for generations to come. It is a legacy of love, support, and security that resonates far beyond the walls of the family home. It's about laying the groundwork for a brighter future, not just for the child, but for society as a whole. A future where individuals are equipped with the emotional intelligence, resilience, and compassion to build a better world. The investment is considerable, but the returns are immeasurable, making this the most significant endeavor a parent can undertake. It's a testament to the power of mindful parenting, and its enduring legacy. It's the bedrock of a brighter tomorrow.

ELEVEN

POSITIVE OUTCOMES OF MINDFUL PARENTING

The previous chapters have explored the potential pitfalls of neglecting a child's emotional and social development, emphasizing the far-reaching consequences of a fractured foundation. But the story doesn't end there. Just as a neglected garden withers, a nurtured one blossoms, revealing the breathtaking beauty of its potential. Mindful parenting, the conscious and intentional cultivation of a child's well-being, yields a harvest of positive outcomes that extend far beyond childhood's fleeting years. It's an investment that pays dividends throughout life, shaping not only the child's destiny but the tapestry of their relationships and contributions to the world.

The most immediate and perhaps most significant benefit of mindful parenting is the fostering of robust mental health.

Children raised with consistent love, understanding, and secure attachment develop a strong sense of self-worth and resilience. They learn to navigate the inevitable ups and downs of life with a greater degree of emotional stability.

They are less likely to succumb to anxiety, depression, or other mental health challenges that plague many adults who lacked the emotional scaffolding provided by mindful

parenting. This isn't to say that mindful parenting is a shield against all adversity; life's inevitable storms will still arise.

However, a child equipped with the emotional tools developed through mindful parenting is better prepared to weather these storms, to adapt, and to emerge stronger on the other side. They possess the inner strength to cope with setbacks, the self-awareness to identify their own emotional needs, and the resilience to bounce back from adversity.

This emotional resilience extends beyond simply navigating personal challenges. It translates into stronger, more fulfilling relationships throughout life. Children raised with mindful parenting learn empathy, compassion, and effective communication skills – the cornerstones of healthy

relationships. They develop a capacity for understanding different perspectives, for navigating disagreements constructively, and for fostering genuine connection with others. They're less likely to engage in conflict-driven or manipulative behaviors, and more likely to build relationships based on mutual respect, trust, and understanding. These skills are essential not only for romantic partnerships but also for friendships, family ties, and professional collaborations. They create a ripple effect, extending their positive influence far beyond the immediate family circle.

The impact of mindful parenting on academic achievement is equally significant, though less direct. While it doesn't guarantee straight A's, it creates an environment conducive to learning and growth. A child who feels secure, loved, and understood is more likely to be engaged and motivated in their studies. They are more likely to approach challenges with curiosity and perseverance, rather than fear and avoidance. The emotional stability fostered by mindful parenting allows children to focus better, to manage stress more effectively, and to approach academic tasks with a greater sense of confidence and self-belief. This isn't about pressuring children to achieve high grades; rather, it's about creating an environment where they can reach their full potential, free from the crippling anxiety of parental pressure.

Moreover, mindful parenting lays the groundwork for greater life satisfaction. This isn't simply about accumulating material wealth or achieving professional success, although those can be positive byproducts. It's about cultivating a sense of purpose, meaning, and fulfillment in life. Children raised with mindful parenting develop a stronger sense of their own values, passions, and aspirations. They are more likely to pursue their goals with determination and resilience, knowing they have a supportive network to lean on during challenging times. They are better equipped to navigate life's complexities, to make informed decisions, and to create a life that aligns with their values and aspirations. This sense of purpose and fulfillment contributes significantly to overall well-being and happiness throughout adulthood.

Beyond the individual benefits, mindful parenting has profound societal implications. By fostering emotionally intelligent, resilient, and compassionate individuals, it contributes to a healthier, more empathetic society. Children raised with mindful parenting are more likely to become engaged citizens, contributing positively to their communities and working towards a better future. They are less likely to engage in risky behaviors, less prone to violence or substance abuse, and more likely to act with integrity and compassion. This isn't merely a utopian ideal; it's a demonstrable outcome of nurturing children within a supportive and loving environment. The cumulative effect of mindful parenting across generations can lead to a more peaceful, prosperous, and harmonious society.

The benefits extend even further. Mindful parenting fosters a strong sense of self-efficacy in children. They learn to believe in their own capabilities, to set goals, and to persevere in the face of adversity. This sense of self-efficacy is a powerful predictor of success in all areas of life, from academic achievement to career advancement to personal relationships. Children who believe in their ability to overcome challenges are more likely to take risks, to pursue their passions, and to achieve their goals, even when faced with setbacks. This self-belief is a gift that keeps on giving, empowering them to navigate life's complexities with confidence and resilience.

Consider the example of two young adults, both facing the same challenging situation—a job loss. One, raised with mindful parenting, approaches the situation with a sense of calm resolve. They acknowledge the disappointment, but they also recognize their own strengths and resilience. They leverage their support network, actively search for new opportunities, and approach the job search with a proactive and positive attitude. The other, raised in a less nurturing environment, may react with panic, self-doubt, and isolation.

They may struggle to cope with the stress, become overwhelmed by negative emotions, and find it difficult to move forward. This illustrates the profound difference that mindful parenting makes in equipping children with the emotional tools they need to navigate life's inevitable challenges.

Another example showcases the long-term benefits in the realm of relationships. Imagine two individuals, one raised with mindful parenting and the other without. Both enter a romantic relationship. The individual raised with mindful parenting is better equipped to communicate their needs and feelings, to navigate disagreements constructively, and to build a relationship based on mutual respect and understanding. They are more likely to seek compromise, to forgive mistakes, and to nurture the relationship through challenging times. The other individual, lacking the emotional intelligence and communication skills fostered by mindful parenting, may struggle to express themselves effectively, leading to misunderstandings, conflict, and ultimately, relationship breakdown. This highlights the lasting impact of mindful parenting on the quality of intimate relationships and the ability to build lasting bonds based on mutual respect and understanding.

The long-term positive outcomes of mindful parenting are not simply theoretical concepts; they are supported by extensive research in developmental psychology and child development. Numerous studies have shown a strong correlation between secure attachment, emotional regulation, and positive outcomes in adulthood. These studies demonstrate the profound impact of early childhood experiences on a child's emotional, social, and cognitive development, underscoring the importance of mindful parenting in shaping a child's life trajectory. The positive outcomes are not merely anecdotal; they are statistically significant and backed by decades of research.

Finally, it's crucial to remember that mindful parenting is not about perfection. It's about intentionality, about striving to create a loving, supportive, and nurturing environment for a child to flourish. It's about being present, understanding, and responsive to a child's needs, both emotional and physical.

It's about recognizing that mistakes will be made – and learning from them. The journey of mindful parenting is a continuous process of growth and learning, for both parent and child. The rewards, however, are immeasurable – a child equipped to navigate life's challenges with resilience,
confidence, and compassion, a child who contributes positively to the world, and a legacy of love that extends far beyond the walls of the family home. The investment is substantial, but the returns, in terms of a child's well-being and the betterment of society, are truly invaluable. It is an investment in a brighter future, for the child and for the world.

Success in Adulthood

The seeds of success, sown in the fertile ground of a nurturing childhood, bear fruit throughout adulthood.

Children who experience consistent love, support, and guidance from their parents are better equipped to navigate the complexities of adult life. This isn't simply about achieving material success, though that can certainly be a byproduct; it's about cultivating a sense of self-worth, resilience, and emotional intelligence that enables individuals to thrive in all aspects of their lives.

Consider the impact of secure attachment. Children raised in secure environments, where their emotional needs are consistently met, develop a strong sense of self. They understand their value, their worthiness of love and belonging, and possess a confidence that allows them to pursue their goals with vigor and determination. This confidence isn't arrogance; it's a quiet assurance that stems from a deep-seated belief in their own capabilities, fostered by years of unconditional love and support. In contrast, children who experience insecure attachment, characterized by inconsistency, neglect, or emotional unavailability, may struggle with self-doubt and low self-esteem throughout their lives. They may find it difficult to form healthy relationships, trust others, or believe in their own potential.

This can manifest in various ways, from difficulty maintaining stable employment to challenges in forming intimate relationships.

The importance of emotional regulation, a skill often learned in childhood, cannot be overstated. Children who learn healthy ways to cope with emotions – through parental guidance, open communication, and the development of coping mechanisms – are better equipped to manage stress and adversity in adulthood. They are less likely to resort to unhealthy coping mechanisms such as substance abuse, self-harm, or destructive behaviors. They possess the emotional resilience to navigate setbacks, bounce back from
disappointments, and maintain a positive outlook even in the face of challenges. Conversely, children who lack the tools for emotional regulation may struggle with anxiety, depression, and other mental health issues throughout their lives. They may find it difficult to manage stress effectively, leading to burnout, relationship difficulties, and impaired overall functioning.

Strong social skills are another crucial element in the formula for adult success. Children who are raised in environments that encourage social interaction, empathy, and respect for others learn valuable social skills that are essential for navigating the complexities of interpersonal relationships. They learn to communicate effectively, resolve conflicts constructively, and build strong, healthy relationships. This social competence contributes to their success in the workplace, where collaboration and teamwork are often key to professional advancement. It also contributes to their overall well-being, as strong social
connections provide a vital source of support, comfort, and meaning in life. Children who lack these social skills may struggle to build and maintain relationships, which can lead to feelings of isolation and loneliness, hindering their personal and professional growth.

Academic achievement, while not the sole measure of success, is often a significant factor in determining future opportunities. Children from nurturing environments, with parents who prioritize education and provide consistent support, are more likely to succeed academically. This support doesn't just mean providing materials; it involves active participation in their child's education, creating a stimulating learning environment at home, and fostering a love of learning. Such children tend to develop stronger study habits, greater motivation, and a more positive attitude towards education, leading to higher academic achievements and opening doors to further education and career opportunities. Conversely, children who lack this support may struggle academically, potentially limiting their future options. This isn't to say that children from disadvantaged backgrounds cannot achieve success; rather, it emphasizes the significance of parental support and encouragement in overcoming obstacles.

Beyond the tangible measures of success, the impact of a nurturing childhood extends to a person's overall well-being. Individuals raised in loving, supportive environments often possess a greater sense of purpose and meaning in life. They are more likely to be involved in their communities, contributing positively to society. They have a stronger moral compass, guided by the values instilled in them during childhood, and are more likely to exhibit empathy and compassion towards others. This contributes to a greater sense of fulfillment and happiness, which are crucial components of a successful and meaningful life.

However, it's vital to acknowledge that the path to success is not linear, and the impact of childhood experiences is not deterministic. Resilience plays a crucial role. Some individuals, despite facing adverse childhood experiences, manage to overcome challenges and achieve great things. Their resilience, their ability to bounce back from setbacks, may be attributed to innate personality traits, supportive relationships outside the family, or their own determination to overcome adversity. This resilience underscores the importance of fostering not just a nurturing environment but also the development of coping mechanisms and problem- solving skills in children, empowering them to navigate life's inevitable difficulties.

Furthermore, success in adulthood encompasses a wide range of dimensions, not merely professional achievement or financial wealth. It involves healthy relationships, a strong sense of purpose, emotional well-being, and contribution to society. A nurturing childhood provides a strong foundation for achieving success in all these areas, but it's not the only factor. Personal choices, opportunities, and sheer determination also play significant roles in shaping an individual's life trajectory.

Ultimately, the relationship between childhood experiences and adult success is complex and multifaceted. While a nurturing childhood offers significant advantages, it's not a guarantee of success. However, it significantly increases the likelihood of a fulfilling and meaningful life, equipping individuals with the emotional intelligence, resilience, and social skills necessary to navigate the complexities of

adulthood and contribute positively to the world. The investment in mindful parenting, in cultivating a loving and supportive environment, is an investment in a brighter future—for the child, and for society as a whole. It's a legacy that extends far beyond the years of childhood, shaping the trajectory of lives and enriching the fabric of our communities. The enduring power of a nurtured childhood is a testament to the profound impact of love, guidance, and understanding on the human spirit, a beacon of hope

illuminating the path towards a more successful and meaningful adulthood. The tapestry of life, woven with threads of love and care, is a beautiful and resilient creation, capable of weathering life's storms and blossoming into a life of purpose and fulfillment.

Breaking the Cycle

The legacy of parenting extends far beyond the formative years. The choices we make as parents, the patterns we establish, often echo through generations. A child raised in an environment lacking consistent affection, clear boundaries, and open communication may unknowingly replicate these dynamics in their own adult relationships and family life. This isn't to assign blame; rather, it's to acknowledge the powerful influence of early experiences on future behavior and to understand how we can consciously interrupt these cycles. Mindful parenting, therefore, isn't merely about raising well-adjusted children; it's about

building a healthier future for families for generations to come.

Understanding the mechanics of these intergenerational patterns is key to breaking free. Imagine a family where emotional expression has been suppressed for generations.

Parents might avoid open conversations about feelings, opting instead for a stiff upper lip approach. Their children, observing this behavior, might internalize the same emotional restraint, carrying it into their own adult relationships. This could manifest as difficulty communicating needs, suppressed emotions leading to resentment, or a reluctance to seek help when struggling.

The cycle continues unless conscious effort is made to disrupt it.

Breaking this cycle begins with self-awareness. Parents need to honestly assess their own upbringing and identify any unhealthy patterns they might unknowingly be perpetuating. Did your parents struggle with addiction, conflict resolution, or emotional regulation? Recognizing these inherited patterns is the first crucial step toward making conscious changes. It's about acknowledging the influence of the past without becoming a victim of it. This process isn't easy; it requires introspection, honesty, and a willingness to confront difficult truths about one's family history. This self- reflection, however, is essential for creating a different future.

Once we recognize these patterns, the next step involves actively choosing different approaches. If you grew up in a household where communication was limited, actively prioritize open and honest dialogue with your children.

Encourage them to express their feelings, even the uncomfortable ones. Validate their emotions, demonstrating empathy and understanding. This fosters a safe space where children feel comfortable sharing their thoughts and feelings without fear of judgment or reprimand. Creating this environment of open communication is a powerful antidote to the silence and suppression that can plague generations.

Similarly, if your childhood lacked clear boundaries, strive to establish healthy limits for your own children. This doesn't mean being overly strict or authoritarian; it means setting reasonable expectations and enforcing them consistently. Children thrive on structure and predictability; it provides them with a sense of security and helps them learn self-discipline. Consistent boundaries, fairly and lovingly enforced, teach children responsibility, respect for rules, and self-regulation – skills crucial for healthy
development and long-term success. It's about finding a balance between freedom and responsibility, empowering children to make choices within a defined framework.

The impact of technology also plays a significant role in perpetuating or interrupting these cycles. Over-reliance on screens can create a sense of isolation and detachment, hindering the development of crucial social skills. Mindful parenting in the digital age requires conscious effort to limit screen time, prioritize face-to-face interactions, and foster meaningful connections within the family. Engaging in family activities, playing games, having dinner together –these simple acts build strong bonds and create lasting
memories. These shared experiences contribute significantly to a child's emotional well-being and sense of belonging.

Furthermore, mindful parenting involves addressing the issue of emotional regulation. Children often mirror their parents' responses to stress and conflict. If parents react with anger or avoidance, children may learn to manage their own emotions in unhealthy ways. Instead, parents should model healthy coping mechanisms, teaching children how to identify, express, and regulate their emotions. This might involve teaching relaxation techniques, practicing mindfulness, or engaging in open conversations about
feelings. The goal is to equip children with the tools they need to navigate life's inevitable challenges with resilience and emotional maturity.

Beyond the immediate family dynamic, breaking the cycle also extends to seeking support when needed.

Acknowledging that parenting is challenging and that it's okay to seek help is vital. This might involve connecting with support groups, therapists, or other parents who share similar experiences. Seeking professional guidance isn't a sign of weakness; it's a testament to the commitment to raising healthy, well-adjusted children. It provides invaluable tools and perspectives that can be instrumental in breaking generational patterns and building a stronger, more supportive family unit.

Consider the case of a young mother named Sarah. Growing up, Sarah witnessed frequent, explosive arguments between her parents, marked by harsh words and emotional distance. As a result, she struggled to form healthy relationships, often replicating the conflict patterns she had observed in her childhood. However, through therapy and conscious effort, Sarah recognized the impact of her past experiences and made a deliberate choice to parent differently. She prioritized open communication with her children, creating a safe space for them to express their emotions without judgment. She taught them healthy conflict-resolution techniques and modeled appropriate responses to stress. As a result, Sarah's children developed strong emotional intelligence and were better equipped to navigate challenges in their own lives. They exhibited healthier communication styles and conflict resolution skills than Sarah had experienced in her own childhood. This is a powerful testament to the impact of mindful parenting and the ability to break unhealthy cycles.

Another example is Mark, whose father was emotionally unavailable and dismissive. Mark, in turn, struggled to express his own feelings and build intimacy in his relationships. He recognized this pattern and sought support from a therapist, who helped him understand the roots of his emotional struggles. With increased self-awareness and the guidance of a professional, Mark made a conscious decision to be more present and emotionally available for his children. He actively engaged in conversations with them, showed empathy, and encouraged open expression of feelings. He prioritized quality time with his family and modeled healthy communication patterns. The result was a vastly different family dynamic compared to his own childhood, marked by strong communication and healthy emotional bonds.

The journey of breaking the cycle of unhealthy parenting patterns is not linear; it requires sustained effort, patience, and a willingness to learn and adapt. There will be setbacks and challenges along the way. However, the reward – a family characterized by healthy relationships, strong communication, and emotional well-being – is invaluable.

Mindful parenting is an ongoing process, a commitment to continuous growth and learning. It's about creating a legacy of love, understanding, and emotional resilience that extends beyond our own children, shaping future generations for the better. It's about weaving a new narrative, one that replaces old patterns with healthier, more fulfilling connections. The power to change the course of family history rests in our hands, offering the profound opportunity to create a brighter future for those who come after. This transformative journey, demanding yet rewarding, underscores the enduring legacy of mindful parenting – a legacy of love, connection, and lasting positive impact across generations.

TWELVE

A Brighter Future for Families

The seeds of change, once sown, possess an undeniable power to sprout and blossom, transforming the landscape of family dynamics across generations. The journey towards mindful parenting, though demanding, ultimately paves the way for a brighter future, not just for our children, but for the entire family constellation. This is not merely about fixing immediate behavioral issues or achieving academic success; it's about fostering a deep-rooted sense of security, belonging, and emotional resilience within the family unit.

This translates into stronger, healthier relationships – not only between parents and children, but also among siblings, extended family, and even future generations.

Consider the ripple effect of a single act of mindful parenting. A parent choosing to actively listen to their child's anxieties, instead of dismissing them, creates a space for open communication. This, in turn, fosters trust and encourages the child to seek guidance and support in future challenges. This trust becomes the foundation upon which healthy relationships are built – relationships characterized by empathy, understanding, and a willingness to communicate effectively. As the child grows, they internalize these patterns of interaction, carrying them into their own adult relationships and, eventually, into their own parenting styles.

The benefits extend beyond the immediate family circle. Children raised in supportive, loving environments are more likely to develop strong social skills and healthy emotional regulation. These are vital assets in navigating the complexities of life, enabling them to form meaningful connections with peers, colleagues, and partners. They are better equipped to handle stress, build resilience, and overcome adversity – characteristics that contribute to overall well-being and success. The positive influence ripples outwards, influencing their friendships, theirworkplaces, and even their communities. The legacy of mindful parenting isn't confined to the home; it permeates every aspect of a child's life and beyond.

Furthermore, the long-term impact of mindful parenting transcends individual well-being, shaping societal structures and cultural norms. When children are raised with a sense of empathy, respect, and understanding, they are more likely to become contributing members of society. They are more likely to embrace diversity, challenge injustice, and contribute to the collective good. They are less prone to aggression, violence, and destructive behaviors, fostering a safer and more harmonious environment for everyone. This isn't a utopian ideal; it's a realistic outcome of nurturing a generation rooted in emotional intelligence and social responsibility.

The transformation isn't solely dependent on parental actions. It necessitates a shift in societal expectations and supports. This requires a collective effort – from schools, communities, and governmental bodies – to create environments that nurture healthy child development.

Schools that prioritize emotional literacy and social- emotional learning, for instance, can significantly contribute to a child's overall well-being. Communities that offer accessible mental health services and family support programs further strengthen the protective factors around children and families. Governmental policies that prioritize affordable childcare, parental leave, and accessible
healthcare can significantly alleviate the pressures on families, allowing them to focus on nurturing their children.

The concept of a "village raising a child" holds true even in today's modern context. While the traditional structure of extended family support may have shifted, we can still cultivate a sense of collective responsibility for the well-being of our children. This involves fostering strong community ties, supporting local initiatives focused on child development, and engaging in open dialogues about the challenges and rewards of parenting. It also demands a societal shift away from the pressures of material success and towards a greater emphasis on the importance of family and community.

Mindful parenting is not a destination; it's a continuous journey of learning, adapting, and growing. It requires self-reflection, honest introspection, and a willingness to challenge our own preconceived notions about parenting. It's about recognizing our limitations, seeking guidance when needed, and continuously striving to become better parents.

This process is enhanced through a support network of friends, family, and professional resources. Support groups, therapy, and parenting workshops offer invaluable opportunities for parents to share their experiences, learn from others, and receive guidance from experts. The investment in our own personal growth as parents is a vital component in creating a brighter future for our families.

The path to positive change is paved with intentional actions, daily choices that reflect our commitment to mindful parenting. These actions aren't grand gestures; they're the small, everyday moments that add up to make a significant difference. A warm hug before school, a listening ear during a difficult moment, a shared family meal, a game of catch in the park – these seemingly insignificant interactions are the building blocks of a strong and loving family. They establish a pattern of connection, trust, and mutual respect, shaping the emotional landscape of the family and influencing generations to come.

Technological advancements, while offering immense convenience, also present significant challenges to mindful parenting. The overreliance on screens, the constant distractions of social media, and the ease with which children can access inappropriate content necessitate conscious effort to establish healthy boundaries and cultivate mindful engagement with technology. This includes setting screen time limits, engaging in family activities that don't involve screens, and actively engaging in conversations with children about responsible technology use. It's about finding a balance that leverages the benefits of technology while mitigating its potential negative effects.

Financial stability is undeniably important for a family's well-being, but it shouldn't come at the expense of genuine connection and emotional support. The prioritizing of material possessions over the emotional needs of children can have profound and lasting consequences. Mindful parenting recognizes the intrinsic value of time spent with children, of genuine interactions that build strong bonds and foster emotional growth. This doesn't necessitate lavish spending; rather, it emphasizes the importance of quality time spent together, of creating shared experiences, and of building lasting memories that nourish the child's emotional development.

The long-term impact of mindful parenting extends even beyond the family unit, impacting the broader community and societal structures. Children raised with a strong sense of empathy, compassion, and social responsibility are more likely to become engaged and active citizens, contributing to their communities and working towards a more just and equitable society. They are better equipped to navigate the challenges of adulthood, build healthy relationships, and contribute positively to the world around them. The collective effect of numerous mindful parenting choices creates a ripple effect of positive change, transforming not only individual families, but society as a whole.

The transformation requires a collective commitment, a concerted effort from individuals, communities, and societal institutions. It's a shared responsibility to cultivate an environment where children thrive, where families flourish, and where the legacy of mindful parenting is passed down through generations. This involves creating supportive communities, advocating for policies that support families, and fostering a culture that prioritizes the emotional well-being of children. It's a journey that requires sustained effort, ongoing learning, and a commitment to creating a brighter future for families, building a legacy of love, connection, and enduring positive impact across generations. The power to reshape family dynamics, to break cycles of unhealthy patterns, and to build a brighter future lies within our reach, awaiting the conscious choices and collective efforts of mindful parents. The rewards – stronger families, healthier communities, and a more compassionate society – are immeasurable.

Reframing the Narrative of Parenting

We've journeyed together through the complexities of modern parenting, exploring the hidden cracks that can fracture a child's foundation. We've examined the pressures of juggling careers, the insidious influence of screens, the pitfalls of permissive parenting, and the dangers of outsourcing the vital work of raising a child to technology. We've looked at the warning signs – behavioral issues, social and emotional deficits, academic struggles, and even physical health indicators – that can signal underlying problems. We've discussed the crucial role of mindful parenting, the power of unconditional love, and the

importance of effective communication and boundary- setting. We've emphasized the need to redefine success, moving beyond material wealth to prioritize emotional well-being and the cultivation of emotional intelligence. We've delved into navigating the digital world responsibly, building resilience in our children, and strengthening the bonds within our families. We've even addressed the vital importance of seeking professional help when needed, acknowledging that asking for support is a sign of strength, not weakness.

But this isn't just about identifying problems and offering solutions; it's about a fundamental shift in perspective, a call to revolutionize how we approach the incredible responsibility of raising the next generation. This chapter is about reframing the narrative of parenting itself. For too long, we've been bombarded with messages that equate success with material wealth, that measure parenting

prowess by the size of our bank accounts rather than the depth of our connections. We've been sold a simplified version of parenting – a one-size-fits-all approach that often falls short of the nuanced realities of raising a child in today's complicated world.

We've been conditioned to believe that the best parents are those who tirelessly chase the elusive goal of "perfection,"often at the expense of their own well-being and the genuine connection they need to foster with their children. This relentless pursuit of an unattainable ideal often leads to feelings of inadequacy, guilt, and ultimately, burnout. It sets an unrealistic standard, making us feel like failures when we inevitably fall short. This relentless pressure not only impacts parents but also creates a ripple effect, harming the very children we strive so hard to protect.

The reality is, parenting is messy, unpredictable, and profoundly challenging. It's filled with moments of joy and overwhelming exhaustion, of immense pride and crushing disappointment. There is no instruction manual, no magic formula, no guarantee of success. What we need is a paradigm shift, a conscious decision to move away from the unrealistic expectations of the "perfect parent" myth and towards a more compassionate, realistic, and ultimately, more effective approach. It's about embracing the

imperfections, acknowledging our limitations, and learning to navigate the complexities of parenthood with grace, self-compassion, and unwavering love.

This reframing begins with a fundamental understanding of what truly matters. It's not about having the biggest house, the most expensive clothes, or the perfect social media feed. It's about creating a nurturing environment where children feel safe, loved, and unconditionally accepted. It's about fostering a deep, meaningful connection that transcends material possessions and societal expectations. It's about being present, truly present, not just physically, but emotionally and mentally engaged in our children's lives.

Consider the countless hours parents spend scrolling through social media, comparing themselves to others, and inadvertently modeling a life of superficiality and instant gratification. What message does this send to our children?

Are we inadvertently teaching them that validation comes from external sources, from likes and followers, rather than from within? This is where the true power of reframing lies –in actively choosing to disconnect from the noise and reconnect with what truly matters: the profound bond between parent and child.

This requires a conscious effort to prioritize quality time over quantity. It means putting down our phones, turning off the television, and engaging in meaningful activities with our children. It means actively listening to them, validating their feelings, and providing them with the emotional support they need to navigate the challenges of life. It means teaching them the importance of self-compassion, resilience, and emotional regulation, skills that will serve them well throughout their lives.

The reframing of the parenting narrative also involves challenging the societal pressures that often undermine our efforts. We need to advocate for policies that support families, such as affordable childcare, paid parental leave, and flexible work arrangements. We need to create communities that offer support and understanding, where parents feel empowered to ask for help without fear of judgment. We must create a cultural shift that prioritizes the well-being of children and families above all else.

Consider the impact of a culture that often glorifies overachievement and prioritizes academic success above emotional health. How many children are struggling silently, burdened by unrealistic expectations and the pressure to perform? How many parents are sacrificing their own well-being in the pursuit of a fleeting sense of accomplishment? We need to challenge this narrative, to create a culture that values empathy, compassion, and emotional intelligence just as much as academic achievement. We need to raise children who are resilient, emotionally intelligent, and capable of navigating the complexities of the world with grace and compassion.

This isn't just about individual change; it's about collective action. We need to support each other, share our experiences, and create a supportive network where parents feel empowered to seek help and to celebrate their successes, however small. We need to challenge the stigma surrounding mental health and encourage open conversations about the challenges of parenting. We need to create a world where parents feel supported, empowered, and confident in their ability to raise happy, healthy, and well-adjusted children.

The journey of parenting is a marathon, not a sprint. There will be setbacks, challenges, and moments of doubt. But by reframing the narrative, by focusing on the essential elements of connection, support, and unconditional love, we can create a path toward healthier, more fulfilling relationships with our children. Remember that seeking help is a sign of strength, not weakness. We are all on this journey together, and by working together, we can create a brighter future for our families and for generations to come. Embrace the journey, embrace the messiness, embrace the love. The reward is immeasurable. The investment is in the future, a future built on the solid foundation of mindful parenting, a future where the hidden cracks are mended, and the bonds of love endure. This isn't just about fixing a crack; it's about building a legacy of love.

Investing in the Future

The journey we've undertaken together—exploring the hidden cracks that can appear in a child's foundation—has not been easy. We've navigated treacherous terrain, confronting uncomfortable truths about modern parenting and the pressures that often overshadow the most essential aspects of raising children. But as we stand at this juncture, poised on the precipice of a new understanding, it's time to shift our focus from identifying the problems to actively investing in solutions. This isn't simply about patching up cracks; it's about building a robust, resilient foundation for our children's futures.

This investment isn't measured in dollars and cents, although financial security undoubtedly plays a role. The true currency of this investment is time, attention, and unwavering emotional commitment. It's about recognizing that the most valuable gift you can give your child is not a lavish toy or a technologically advanced gadget, but the unwavering presence of a loving, engaged parent. It's the presence that fosters a secure attachment, a strong sense of self, and the resilience to face the inevitable challenges life throws their way.

Consider the intangible riches you bequeath when you dedicate time to truly *seeing* your child. Not just observing their actions, but actively listening to their thoughts and feelings, validating their emotions, even when they're messy or confusing. This means setting aside the distractions—the emails, the social media notifications, the never-ending to-do list—and truly being present. It means creating space for meaningful conversations, fostering open communication, and building a relationship based on trust and mutual respect. This isn't about perfection; it's about presence.

Remember those seemingly insignificant moments: reading a bedtime story with genuine enthusiasm, sharing a quiet moment of laughter, offering a comforting hug when tears fall. These seemingly small acts are the building blocks of a strong and loving parent-child relationship, laying the groundwork for a secure and confident adult. These moments become the anchors that will hold them steady when faced with storms in later life. They provide the safety net that allows exploration, risk-taking, and the development of their own unique personalities.

Think about the ways you can nurture their emotional intelligence. Help them understand and manage their feelings, teaching them to identify and express emotions in healthy ways. This involves creating a safe space where they feel comfortable sharing their vulnerabilities without fear of judgment or ridicule. Guide them in developing empathy and compassion, fostering their ability to connect with and

understand the feelings of others. This is an essential skill that will serve them well throughout their lives, shaping their relationships and their ability to navigate the complexities of the social world.

The investment in their future also involves actively shaping their values. Children are incredibly perceptive, absorbing the lessons taught through actions as much as through words.

What values are you modeling? Are you demonstrating kindness, honesty, integrity, and empathy? Are you showing them the importance of perseverance, resilience, and a commitment to personal growth? These are not merely abstract concepts; they are the guiding principles that will shape their moral compass and their choices throughout life.

The values you instill will determine the kind of adults they become.

Beyond the emotional realm, there's the crucial element of intellectual stimulation. This doesn't necessarily mean pushing them toward academic excellence at all costs. It's about fostering a lifelong love of learning, encouraging curiosity, and providing them with opportunities to explore their interests. Support their passions, whether it's playing a musical instrument, writing stories, or building intricate structures. Engage in intellectually stimulating conversations, read together, visit museums and libraries—provide a rich and diverse environment that nurtures their cognitive development. This creates a pathway to lifelong learning, making them self-sufficient and enthusiastic in their intellectual endeavors.

Crucially, this investment necessitates a conscious effort to disconnect from technology and reconnect with each other.

We've discussed the dangers of excessive screen time, the ways in which it can erode face-to-face interactions and hinder emotional development. Limit screen time, creating family rituals and activities that involve direct engagement and shared experiences. Family dinners, games nights, outdoor adventures—these are the moments that build lasting memories and strengthen family bonds. These shared experiences are essential in fostering a cohesive unit where every member feels seen, heard, and valued.

Furthermore, it's critical to cultivate a strong sense of community. Children thrive in environments where they feel connected to something larger than themselves. This might involve volunteering as a family, participating in community events, or simply engaging with their neighbors. Fostering a sense of belonging and social responsibility not only builds their empathy and understanding of the world, but also teaches them the importance of contributing to something greater than their individual needs. This prepares them for the collaborative spirit required in the modern world and allows them to grow into socially conscious individuals.

Finally, remember that this investment is a marathon, not a sprint. There will be moments of frustration, times when you feel overwhelmed or inadequate. There will be setbacks, challenges, and the inevitable bumps along the road. But the journey itself is a crucial part of the process. The struggles, the triumphs, the moments of shared laughter and shared tears—these are the experiences that shape both you and your child. Embrace the imperfections, learn from your mistakes, and never lose sight of the ultimate goal: to nurture a loving, supportive, and enriching environment where your child can flourish.

This isn't about ahieving a perfect outcome; it's about creating a strong foundation built on love, understanding, and a genuine commitment to your child's well-being. It's about investing in the person they are, the person they are becoming, and the person they will one day be. It's an investment that will yield immeasurable returns, enriching not only their lives, but your own as well. The legacy you create—a legacy of love, connection, and unwavering support—will endure long after the years of parenting have passed, echoing through generations to come. This is the legacy of mindful parenting; this is the future we build together. The investment in their future is an investment in your own; it's an investment in a brighter tomorrow.

Embrace the journey. The reward is a lifetime of love and connection, a bond that transcends time and circumstance. The investment is worth far more than any material wealth; it's priceless.

Creating a Legacy of Love

The journey of parenting is a marathon, not a sprint. We've discussed the pitfalls, the hidden cracks that can fracture a child's foundation. We've acknowledged the pressures of modern life, the seductive allure of screens, and the insidious creep of prioritizing material success over genuine connection. But now, standing on the other side of those acknowledgments, we must look forward, towards the future we are building, brick by mindful brick, with the mortar of unconditional love. This is not merely about raising well-adjusted children; it's about cultivating a legacy of love that ripples outwards, touching generations to come.

Consider the legacy you want to leave behind. Is it one of overflowing bank accounts and impressive achievements, or one of warmth, laughter, shared memories, and a profound sense of belonging? The answer, I believe, is self-evident. While material success can provide comfort and security, it pales in comparison to the enduring power of love, the kind of love that transcends time and circumstance, the kind of love that nurtures the soul. This is the legacy we build not just for our children but for ourselves. It is a legacy that provides a comforting bedrock for navigating life's
complexities.

Building this legacy requires conscious effort, a daily commitment to presence and connection. It means putting down the phone, silencing the notifications, and truly seeing your child. It means engaging in their world, listening to their anxieties and celebrating their triumphs, even the small ones. It's about fostering a sense of security, a safe space where they feel loved, understood, and accepted, regardless of their imperfections or mistakes. This unconditional love is the cornerstone of a strong, healthy relationship. It is the foundation upon which their self-esteem, resilience, and capacity for empathy are built.

Think about the moments that define your own childhood. Were they moments of material abundance, or moments of connection, laughter, and shared experiences? Chances are, it's the memories of love and connection that hold the most weight, that still resonate within you. These memories shape who you are, influencing your values, your beliefs, and your approach to life. The memories you create with your
children will have the same profound impact on them. This is the power of legacy; it shapes the tapestry of future generations, influencing their values, beliefs, and overall well-being.

This isn't about creating perfect children; perfection is an illusion, a mirage in the desert of parenting. It's about raising compassionate, resilient, and emotionally intelligent individuals who are equipped to navigate the complexities of life with grace and understanding. It's about teaching them the importance of empathy, kindness, and respect—not just for others, but for themselves as well. This self-respect, cultivated through a secure and loving childhood, will serve as their compass, guiding them through the storms of life. It provides them a stable core, helping them navigate difficulties and maintain perspective.

Creating this legacy requires more than just words; it demands action. It involves actively participating in your child's life, being present in their moments of joy and sorrow. It means engaging in meaningful conversations, listening without judgment, and offering support without reservation. It's about making time for family rituals—dinner together, game nights, reading aloud—moments that create shared memories and strengthen the bonds of connection. These shared experiences weave a rich tapestry of love, creating a lasting impression on a child's developing mind.

Consider the power of storytelling. Sharing your own experiences, both good and bad, helps children learn from your mistakes and celebrate your successes. It demonstrates resilience, demonstrating that setbacks are inevitable, but that overcoming adversity is a fundamental aspect of human experience. By sharing your stories, you create a sense of shared history, a bond that transcends the everyday. This continuity of shared experiences, passed down through generations, builds a powerful sense of belonging and connection.

Remember the importance of modeling healthy behaviors.

Children learn by observing, emulating the actions and attitudes of those they admire. If you prioritize kindness, compassion, and empathy, your children will likely adopt these values as well. Conversely, if you exhibit negativity, anger, or disconnection, your children are more likely to incorporate these behaviors into their own lives. Thus, the importance of self-reflection is paramount. We must strive to live according to the principles we wish to instill in our children.

Another critical aspect of building this legacy is fostering a strong sense of community. Children thrive in environments where they feel connected to others, where they have opportunities for social interaction and support. Encourage your child to participate in activities that foster a sense of belonging, whether it's sports teams, clubs, or volunteer work. These external connections enrich their lives, providing a network of support and understanding that complements the love and support they receive at home. This integrated approach, encompassing both familial and external relationships, creates a robust support system, crucial for emotional well-being and resilience.

Furthermore, understand that creating a legacy of love is not a passive process; it requires consistent effort and commitment. It's a continuous journey, one that evolves and adapts as your children grow and change. There will be challenges, setbacks, and moments of frustration. But amidst these difficulties, remember the importance of your role as a guide, a mentor, a beacon of love and support. Your unwavering love and unwavering support serve as a constant, a grounding force for your child, providing them the security to explore and grow.

Finally, remember that your legacy isn't just about your children; it's about the ripple effect that your actions have on future generations. The values, beliefs, and behaviors you instill in your children will shape their relationships, their careers, and their approach to life. They will, in turn, pass these values on to their own children, creating a chain of love and compassion that extends far beyond your lifetime. This continuity of values and beliefs strengthens the fabric of family and community, creating a legacy of positive influence that spans generations. This is the true power of mindful parenting, the creation of a legacy built not on material possessions, but on the enduring power of love, connection, and unwavering support. It's an investment that returns immeasurable value – a brighter future for your children, and indeed, for all generations to come. It's a legacy worth pursuing, a legacy worth cherishing.

The Power of Collective Change

The individual journey of mindful parenting, while crucial, is only one piece of a much larger, more impactful puzzle.

We've explored the hidden cracks that can develop in a child's foundation, the subtle ways in which societal pressures and technological advancements can undermine the parent-child bond. But the solution isn't simply about individual transformation; it demands a collective shift in our societal understanding of parenting and childhood. We need a village, a community, a supportive network that actively reinforces the principles of mindful parenting, not just within individual families, but across the broader spectrum of society.

Imagine a world where schools prioritize emotional intelligence alongside academic achievement, where teachers are trained to recognize the signs of emotional distress in children and equipped to provide appropriate support. Picture playgrounds that are not just spaces for physical activity but also environments that foster social interaction, cooperation, and conflict resolution. Envision community centers that offer parenting workshops, not just on discipline techniques, but on building strong emotional connections, fostering resilience, and understanding the complexities of child development.

This collective change requires a multi-pronged approach. Firstly, we need a societal shift in our values. The relentless pursuit of material success often overshadows the importance of nurturing relationships and investing time in our children. We need to collectively redefine success, recognizing that a child's well-being is not a side effect of material prosperity but its very foundation. This means advocating for policies that support families, such as affordable childcare, parental leave, and flexible work arrangements. It means challenging the pervasive societal pressures that often lead parents to prioritize career advancement over their child's emotional needs.

Secondly, we need to actively challenge the pervasive influence of technology. While technology offers many benefits, its constant presence can be detrimental to a child's development. Excessive screen time, often a default parenting strategy in today's busy world, isolates children, hindering their ability to develop crucial social skills and emotional intelligence. This requires a concerted effort from parents, educators, and policymakers alike. We need to promote media literacy, teaching children and parents to be critical consumers of information and to understand the potential risks associated with excessive screen time. This also involves creating more engaging and enriching offline activities, encouraging physical play, creative pursuits, and social interaction.

Thirdly, and perhaps most importantly, we need to cultivate a culture of empathy and understanding. We need to create a society that recognizes the challenges of parenting and offers support rather than judgment. This means building strong communities, fostering networks of support among parents, and encouraging open and honest conversations about the difficulties of raising children in the modern world. Support groups, online forums, and community-based initiatives can provide parents with a safe space to share their experiences, learn from one another, and receive guidance from professionals. This shift in societal perception is crucial because it creates a safety net for parents, allowing them to seek help without fear of stigma or criticism.

Consider the impact of creating comprehensive parenting education programs, integrated into the curriculum of schools and readily accessible to the wider community.

These programs should not just focus on the technical aspects of childcare, but also delve into the emotional intricacies of parent-child relationships, conflict resolution, and fostering emotional well-being. They should explore different parenting styles, their implications, and equip parents with the tools to adopt a mindful approach. Imagine a world where these programs are as widely accepted and attended as driver's education—a necessary and essential component of responsible adulthood.

Furthermore, we need to invest in mental health services specifically tailored to children and adolescents. Early intervention is crucial in addressing potential behavioral and emotional problems. This includes increasing access to mental health professionals, providing training for educators and community workers to recognize signs of distress, and creating a culture where seeking help is seen as a sign of strength, not weakness. A society that truly prioritizes children's well-being would readily invest in such resources, ensuring that every child has access to the support they need, regardless of their socioeconomic background.

The role of media in shaping our perceptions of parenting cannot be overstated. We need to critically examine the messages conveyed through television, movies, and social media. Often, these portrayals present an unrealistic and idealized version of parenting, placing undue pressure on parents and perpetuating harmful stereotypes. A more responsible approach would involve showcasing diverse parenting styles, highlighting the challenges and joys of raising children, and promoting a message of empathy and understanding.

The transition to this more supportive and mindful parenting society won't happen overnight. It will require sustained effort from individuals, communities, and policymakers alike. We need to engage in open dialogue, share our experiences, and advocate for policies that support families and children. We need to challenge outdated norms and create a new paradigm where nurturing and supportive relationships are not just ideal goals but societal norms.

The creation of this supportive ecosystem is not merely altruistic; it's an investment in the future. By fostering healthier, more resilient children, we create a stronger, more compassionate society. This is not simply about improving the lives of children; it's about creating a better future for all. A collective commitment to mindful parenting translates into a reduction in social problems stemming from childhood trauma and neglect – leading to a healthier, more productive workforce, stronger communities, and a more harmonious society as a whole. The benefits extend far beyond the individual family unit, reaching into the very fabric of our social structures.

This collective action isn't about imposing a single, uniform parenting style. It's about fostering a shared understanding of the importance of mindful parenting, promoting open communication and support among parents, and creating a societal structure that actively supports families in their efforts to raise happy, healthy, and well-adjusted children.

This involves embracing diversity, respecting individual choices, and recognizing that there is no one-size-fits-all approach to parenting. The goal is not conformity, but a shared commitment to fostering a nurturing environment for every child.

The power of collective change lies in its ability to create a ripple effect. When one community embraces mindful parenting, it inspires others to do the same. When one school prioritizes emotional well-being, it sets a precedent for other schools to follow. This snowball effect, driven by shared values and a collective commitment to change, can transform our society, creating a brighter future for generations to come. It is a long-term investment, one that requires patience, perseverance, and a unwavering belief in the potential for positive change. But the rewards—a society that values its children, fosters their growth, and supports their well-being—are immeasurable. This is not just a call to action; it is a call to create a legacy of love, support, and enduring well-being for all. It is a legacy we can—and must—build together.

Embracing the Journey

The weight of responsibility can feel crushing sometimes.

The constant pressure to be the perfect parent, the endless stream of conflicting advice, the fear of making mistakes—it can all feel overwhelming. But remember, you are not alone. Every parent, regardless of their background or experience, grapples with these challenges. The journey of parenting is not a race to the finish line; it's a marathon, filled with ups and downs, twists and turns. And just like any marathon, there will be moments of exhaustion, doubt, and even despair. But there will also be moments of breathtaking beauty, profound connection, and unwavering love.

Allow yourself to feel those difficult emotions. Don't try to suppress them or pretend they don't exist. Acknowledge them, process them, and then let them go. Holding onto negative emotions only adds to the burden, hindering your ability to be fully present for your child. Find healthy ways to cope with stress, whether it's through exercise, meditation, spending time in nature, or connecting with supportive friends and family. Remember that self-care is not selfish; it's essential. You cannot pour from an empty cup. If you are depleted, you cannot effectively nurture your child.

Seeking help is a sign of strength, not weakness. It takes courage to admit you need support, to acknowledge that you're struggling. Don't be afraid to reach out to your partner, friends, family, or mental health professionals. There are countless resources available to help you navigate the complexities of parenting. Whether it's a parenting class, a support group, or individual therapy, there is help out there.

And seeking that help doesn't mean you've failed; it means you're committed to doing the best you can for your child.

Remember the small victories. Those quiet moments of connection, the shared laughter, the heartfelt conversations—they are the building blocks of a strong parent-child relationship. Focus on those moments, cherish them, and let them fuel you through the challenging times. Celebrate the progress you've made, no matter how small. Acknowledge your efforts, your dedication, and your unwavering love. You are doing your best, and that's enough.

One of the most significant hurdles many parents face is the overwhelming pressure to achieve a specific outcome – the perfect grades, the prestigious college acceptance, the high-flying career. This relentless focus on external achievements often overshadows the importance of nurturing a child's inner world, their emotional well-being, and their sense of self. This pressure, often unconsciously transmitted from society, family, or even our own internalized beliefs, can create unnecessary stress for both parents and children. The relentless pursuit of external validation can lead to anxiety, depression, and a distorted sense of self-worth, especially in children who are not intrinsically motivated to conform to these externally imposed standards.

Instead of focusing solely on external validation, prioritize intrinsic motivation. Cultivate your child's curiosity, nurture their passions, and encourage them to pursue their own interests. Support their dreams, even if they differ from your own expectations. Help them understand the value of effort and perseverance, regardless of the final outcome. Teach them to find joy in the process, not just the result. This shift in perspective will not only reduce stress and anxiety but will also foster a stronger, more resilient child who is comfortable with taking calculated risks and exploring their own capabilities.

Moreover, the societal pressure to project an image of perfection often leaves parents feeling inadequate and isolated. The curated portrayals of idealized family life on social media can intensify this feeling, creating a false narrative that hides the realities of everyday struggles and imperfections. It's crucial to understand that the 'perfect' family is a myth, a construction fueled by unrealistic expectations. Genuine connection, open communication, and unconditional love are far more important than achieving some externally imposed definition of success.

Engage in activities that foster connection and shared experiences. Create opportunities for family bonding, even amidst the chaos of daily life. A simple family dinner, a game night, or even just cuddling on the couch and reading together can strengthen the parent-child bond and create lasting memories. Remember that quality time is more valuable than quantity. Prioritize being present and engaged with your child over merely being physically present.

Put away your phone, turn off the TV, and give your child your undivided attention. Listen actively to what they have to say, even if it seems trivial. Show empathy, understanding, and genuine interest in their thoughts and feelings.

Furthermore, embrace imperfection. Parenting is a messy, unpredictable journey. There will be mistakes, missteps, and moments of regret. Acknowledge these imperfections, learn from them, and move on. Don't let them define you or diminish your worth as a parent. Perfection is an unattainable goal; striving for it only leads to disappointment and frustration. Instead, focus on progress, not perfection. Celebrate your successes, both big and small, and learn from your mistakes. Remember, it's the journey, not the destination, that truly matters.

Finally, let's redefine success in parenting. Instead of measuring success based on external achievements, let's focus on building strong, healthy, and resilient children.

Children who are emotionally intelligent, socially competent, and able to navigate the complexities of life with confidence and compassion. Children who know they are loved unconditionally, who feel safe and secure, and who are equipped with the tools they need to thrive. This is the true measure of success in parenting—raising children who are happy, healthy, and capable of leading fulfilling lives. This journey is a testament to the enduring power of love, patience, and unwavering commitment, and a journey every parent deserves to embrace without the unnecessary pressure of an unattainable ideal.